"*Midwestern Pulp* i
and indictment of t
follows in the footst
Confederacy of Dunces and Don DeLillo's *White Noise* in holding a mirror, however darkly, to banal cultural touchstones, teasing out the "beautiful strangeness" of existence. He takes on the almost Sisyphean task of peering through the normal in search of the sublime. It's a neon-tinged novel calling out from the cultural wilderness of northern Ohio, forcing you to reckon with your own biases and wonder if it was you who missed the point and if you've been thinking about "home" incorrectly all along."

—Will C. Farley, Author of *Big Fish, Or Some Such Nonsense*, *willcfarley.com*

"...Mic Fox sculpts a tensile, living ecosystem, a nebula of collective resilience, profoundly nonsensical ingenuity, and the aporetic relationship between cultural survivalism, nostalgic reverie, and the persistence of the Platonic ideal of homeplace—the Derridean "at home." Therein he lays bare a rich tapestry of straight-up cinematic diegesis and ethnographic fiction truer-than-life because it's totally made up. As trite as that sounds, it slaps...with heart."

—Tim Woods, Your Bartender's Bartender, Chief Juice Wrangler at Gästkellerei Wines

"Feels like the first bite of Joan Vanderhyden's hot dish in the church basement."

—Ian Bush, Vibe Curator at Banshees Ritual

Midwestern Pulp

(A Love Letter to Lake Erie)

—

Mic Fox

Thanks to A.O. & M.F. for the notes and the edits, the real ones for reading it, and the Famly for the inspiration.

The book was typed in Century School Book. Additional fonts include Arial, Avenir Next, Bodoni 72 Oldstyle, Brush Script, Cooper, Cooperplate, Elephant Pro, Jokerman, Papyrus, and Source Sans Pro.

ISBN: 9798711137238

Fort Famly is a Famly LLC property.
Find out more at
fortfamly.com

Bonus Merch and Book Content at fortfamly.com/extra-pulp
Password: aSNAKEcalledMICHAEL

For all the homies holding it down back home

A Disclaimer

I'd like to thank you for attempting to chug through some of these words.

I started writing this with the hope of dissecting and understanding the ideologies and behaviors of Northwest Ohio.

But instead, I ended up with a few interconnected short stories followed by a 200-page narrative written in the style of a long-winded PG-13-year-old. Eh…maybe not PG-13…but only R for language. There's nothing *that* cool in here. I promise.

If that's not what you're looking for, I completely understand. But that's what we've got.

So, without further ado, I'd like to whisk you away to a place between Columbus and Canada, where the sky's as grey as the water and the beer's as cold as the ice you put it in. A place so mildly unhinged that it passes inspection without much inspection at all. A place that's completely fictional and in-no-way-based-in-reality or involving people that I know in real-life…

...

Midwestern Pulp

(A Love Letter to Lake Erie)

...

Mic Fox

Part One

...

Four to Five Freaks

to

Set the Setting

Donnie

It's either 1986 or 2012, and it doesn't matter because this part of the world doesn't change, or age, or respond to normal fluctuations in weather or time or anything like that.

But it's summer in Northwest Ohio and I'm barbacking at an establishment on an island off the coast of Port Clinton. By barbacking, I mean that I am carrying buckets of ice from a shed that houses an ice machine to another building that puts warm beer into said ice and sells said beer to 42-year-old spring breakers. Would it be more efficient and cost-effective to buy refrigerators for said establishment? Sure. But it's 1994 and refrigerators haven't been invented yet.

A large portion of my job is waiting for these giant buckets to fill up with ice. As I wait for my ice, I have to constantly be on the lookout for this man named Donnie.

Donnie is a person who presumably lives on the island, though I have seen a car that looks just like his on the ferry. (He drives a crummy old Buick that he just loves. It has a sticker on the back window that, from a distance, looks like a Freemason's compass. But up close, it's just drawings of male genitals in the shape of a Freemason's compass.) He has a female Blue Nose Pit Bull named Bob Saget. And when people ask what her name is, he loves pretending like he's never heard of the actor, Bob Saget, before.

The issue with Donnie, other than the fact that he's the worst, is that he's constantly trying to steal ice out of the ice machine. He's always stealing ice because this monster of a person is *always* wearing a knee-length fur coat in the middle of the summer.[1]

To say that Donnie is eccentric would both be an understatement and be giving him far too much credit. He has no artistic sensibilities unless you consider perversion an art form.

His perversion has a specific radar for, and gravitation to, overly intoxicated women (and occasionally men) in the throes of a mid-life crisis. Ironically enough, these people seem to have a strange attraction to him after fewer drinks than you'd think. I don't have a rock-solid explanation for this. I'm no scientist. But if I were, I'd recognize and record the following pattern of behaviors:

---

[1] I mean...I've never seen him without it.

Person A (let's call her Donna) walks into our establishment.

I use the word "our" here because the owner of our establishment, Chris, likes us to use first-person plurals while we're at work. He's very intentional about this. I think he probably read about it in some self-helpy sort of business book, but the level of intention leads me to believe that he enjoys the first-person because it allows him to feel like a part of something. I don't think Chris has many friends.

Anyway...

Donna walks into our establishment. She has obviously been drinking before entering said establishment. Donna is 49 years young, a mother of two, engaged to her second husband, and on a "low-key bachelorette party with some of her bitches." She is a very classy lady.

I am only kidding.

She orders a relatively obscure-sounding cocktail that's really just a vodka soda with grenadine. (I've seen it called a Dirty Shirley Temple or a Russian Kiss or any number of other dumb names.)

She scolds the bartender for not knowing what she's talking about, then teaches her how to make the drink.

At this point, our hero, Donnie, catches a change in the air. His nose picks up the fragrance of "regretful decisions from years gone by." He then tunes his ear to a certain frequency that all Donnas' voices seem to produce.

It seems Donnie isn't affected by any variable in this entire universe, other than the presence of a Donna.

Donnie scans the room—searching for his Donna. While the untrained eye may see a room full of Donnas, Donnie knows the differences and nuances between all archetypes in this bar.

He knows he doesn't stand a chance with Kimberlys or Kelseys.

Barbaras and Dianes would eat him alive.

And let's be honest, Sierras and Ambers would marry him, poison him, and send his Buick into the lake. (Or worse yet, they'd live a relatively normal life back on the mainland and grow old together.)

But Donnas...Donnas are Donnie's sweet spot. And Donnie is Donna's very strange 2–3-day escape from the mediocrity that she's afraid her life has become. (Though if you're ever in the position or state of mind to willingly bring a person like Donnie into your life, your situation is far from mediocre. And it's already far out of your control.)

From this point, Donnie will find a window to approach his Donna. Her initial reaction to his presence is to harden her shell and reject his gaze. (And rightfully so, because addressing Donnie is a critical error in trying to keep him away from you.) But, because Donna is without better judgement (and has been ignored by friends and partners alike), she can't help but enjoy the attention. So, she glances back at him for a fraction of a second, from the other end of the bar.

At this point, anybody who works in the bar can tell you almost exactly where this is going.

Donnie will approach Donna.

He will ask her name.

She will give him a fake name. Let's say, "Brookie." (Donnie also knows that this isn't her name.)

Donnie will laugh and say "Okay, Brookie. What're you drinking?"

Before she can respond, he'll yell to the bartender, "Hey Meg, babe, could you get us two Dirty Shirlies." The bartender's name is Meghan and hates being called "Meg." But Donnie tips well when he's with a Donna and let's be honest, Meghan has been called more horrible things today alone.

Donna secretly loves how forward Donnie's acting. She's never been with a man so confident. Not really. And Donnie's confidence seems to make her more confident, herself. And she loves that. Her friends say she should be more confident. She should be more spontaneous like her friend, Brandy. (When Donnie asked her name, her initial thought was to say "Brandy," but at the last second, she changed her mind. "Brookie." How spontaneous.)

With her newfound confidence, Donna (Brookie) comments on Donnie's drink order.

"What the hell is a Dirty Shirley?" [2]

"Well Miss Brookie...a Dirty Shirley's what you ordered when you first walked in," replies Donnie calmly.

"Well...mister..."

"Johnson," says Donnie "My friends call me Johnson." (Nobody calls him "Johnson" and I'm pretty sure that's not his last name. He always uses a name that could refer to his member. Johnson, Willy, Dick, etc.)

"Well, Mr. Johnson. I'm not drinking a Dirty Shirley."

At this point, the bartender is finished with the drinks and has set them in front of him. (Meghan often stalls on the drinks in an attempt to ruin Donnie's plans, but usually to no avail. He is a master of small talk and can stall for hours, eventually turning it around on the bar and causing enough of a scene to frighten less horrible customers.)

Donnie gestures towards the glasses and says, "If that drink isn't exactly what you want, I'll pay your tab, walk outta here, and you'll never see this face again."

Donna pauses. Not because she's afraid. But because she knows *exactly* where this weekend's going.

They lock eyes. Cheers. And sip their drinks.

Donna is silent. It's the exact drink she ordered. She's impressed. Too impressed. She's never been so impressed in

---

[2] She's being so sassy here. Brookie's a real bad bitch. Not like Donna. Brookie doesn't let a *man* tell her what she wants.

all her days. She fears she'll never be so well taken care of ever again in her life! Poor Donna. Seems like quite the jump.

Donna breaks her silence.

"Hmm..." she says.

"Not bad huh?" Donnie replies, nodding his head.

"And you said you'd pay my tab if this wasn't *exactly* what I wanted?" says Donna, in a way where you can tell that she thinks she's being clever.

"That's right," says Donnie, in a way where we all know *exactly* where this is going.

"Well...this isn't *EXACTLY* what I wanted," she replies playfully.

"Oh yeah? Well what *exactly* DO you want?" he responds.

"Oh, I think you know *EXACTLY* WHAT I WANT."

At which point they are face to face, so close that they are speaking directly into each other's mouths.

Without breaking eye contact, Donnie pulls out two $20 bills and puts them on the bar. Both Donnie and Donna slam their drinks back, keeping eye contact all the while, eye contact approaching the level of a childhood staring contest.

Donna, scared to look away for fear that she may talk herself out of what's to come—but also looking for the love she'd always wished she had as a child. It's as if she's asking him for *pure passion* with her eyes. And despite the fact that she's not seeing it, she persists as if it's in there somewhere. And since she's never experienced anything like this before, maybe this *is* what pure passion feels like.

Donnie, afraid that if he breaks first, Donna may actually recognize what a stupid idea it is to just leave her friends and go off with some weird dude wearing a fur coat on an island in the middle of Lake Erie.

But she breaks first. Not to leave him, but to grab her counterfeit, overly-branded, oversized purse and make eye contact with her friends as if to say, "Don't wait up for me, bitches."

So, they walk out together, arm in arm, Donnie and Donna. Almost in slow motion. Not in a good way, but in a train wreck sort of way. You don't want to see it. You hate to see it. But you're seeing it, and you can't look away.

My first reaction, once they leave, is a sigh of relief. It's a silent "Well, there they go. Glad we don't have to deal with that anymore." But if you think that thought has any validity, you'd be wrong. Because if you hang around this part of the world long enough, you realize that everyone comes back around. Donnie will be back later today. Maybe once more. Maybe twice. But he's definitely behind the building, in the shed, digging through the ice machine with his filthy, filthy hands, right this second.

Tracy

It's 1992. My mother, 20, and my father, just 21, bungee cord me and my car seat to the center console of a 1982 Chrysler LeBaron convertible. I, myself, am 19 months old and quite mature for my age.

We're going to a place called The Horseshoe. People around here call it "Shoes." It's a bar in the shape of a horseshoe (hence the name), and in the middle of the horseshoe-shaped building there are a few picnic tables and a horseshoe pit.[3]

Shoes is a concept that would make more sense in Texas, but here we are, an hour and a half southeast of Detroit, in the middle of a cornfield.

We're here because my parents are meeting up with some friends. Friends they went to high school with. Some of these people are mere acquaintances to me, but some of them I know quite well. These good friends of my parents are the type that I, later in life (when I can talk), will refer to as Uncle Bo or Aunt Deb (these names are just examples. I don't have an Uncle Bo or Aunt Deb.)

---

[3] "Horseshoes" is a game where two teams throw horseshoes back and forth at two metal stakes sticking up out the ground. A "Horseshoe pit" would be the field in which the two teams play "Horseshoes." The object of the game is to get intoxicated with your friends while throwing metal objects.

The Uncle Bos and Aunt Debs of my life are great. They're nice to me. They talk to me like a person, despite the fact that I am a child. They're great. And as a child, other than legal-relation-level family, Bos and Debs may be the only people I truly love.

Now, Uncle Bos and Aunt Debs don't necessarily need to be partners. Uncle Bo and Aunt Deb can function as separate entities. They may not even be close friends. (But if they're not close friends, they are friends by proxy—because of my parents.) The only issue with Uncle Bos and Aunt Debs is that they aren't in the same phase of life as my parents. This isn't a bad thing. It just affects the longevity of my relationship with them. The trajectory of Uncle Bos and Aunt Debs can go in a few different directions.

A. Bo and Deb will entertain the idea of, but later mutually realize that they shouldn't be together. They will keep up with my parents separately, but once my parents have another kid, or Bo and Deb find partners of their own, the amount of time that passes in between our little get-togethers will increase. (Despite the fact that when we do see each other, they say things like, "I'll call you. We need to do this more often.")

B. Bo and Deb will date for longer than they should. They have a great season. A lot of passionate conversations. But all good things come to an end. One of them (and only ONE of them) will be determined to make it work despite the fact that they both know it's probably not in the cards. Things will end dramatically. One of them will end up with a motorcycle (it could be either of them, really), and one of them will end up living at my parents' house for a couple months (could also go either way). But once the drama has subsided, they will abruptly detach from my parents, because they associate my folks and their stability with this former life—a life they're "trying desperately to forget."

C. A few years down the line, Bo and Deb realize that they should be together, after all. Things are great. We meet up with them on a regular basis. They babysit me so my folks can go out. It's great. But after their honeymoon phase is over, they decide that they want to start a family of their own. At this point, I'm probably 5 years old and I've got *at least* two younger siblings (my parents are cornfed-Catholic fertile) and we're happy to hang with Bo and Deb's new baby…for a bit. But I've got t-ball…I'm in kindergarten…I've got a full-time job…I've got kids of my own for Chrissake. We're busy. And Deb wants to move back to Sandusky to be closer to her parents. Sandusky's not far, but we still don't see them as often. And when we do see them, they say things like, "I'll call you. We need to do this more often."

I miss my Uncle Bos and Aunt Debs. Those were good times. But like I said, all good things must come to an end. And honestly, around here, "ALL GOOD THINGS MUST COME TO AN END" could be a banner that hangs on an overpass off I-75. And hell, if it's a pedestrian overpass, the high school cheerleaders could spell it out with colorful plastic cups stuck in the chain-link fence. That'd look real nice.

So, I'm at Shoes with my parents, Bo, Deb, and a few other randos. It's a strangely warm day in late winter. St. Patrick's Day decorations are up around the bar. Shiny vinyl clovers cover the windows around the entrance. And as a one-and-a-half-year-old, I love shiny vinyl clovers. Honestly, they're the only reason I come to this place—as a baby, I'm not strong enough for horseshoes and once they started carding me at the bar, I thought, "forget this!"—but the decorations are great.

Truth be told, it's probably a little cold to be sitting outside, but after being cooped up all winter, people will do anything to get out of the house. It's one of those rare, only *partly* cloudy days and plenty of other people appeared to have the same idea we did because the place is slammed. I see my mother look at my father with her "Are we actually going to go in there with a baby right now?" sort of face. My father looks back at her with his "Are you going to make me tell our friends that we're not showing up to my own birthday party because you don't want to take our baby into the bar?" face. There's a standoff for a second, but my father takes control of the situation. He knows that he's accepting liability if my mother has a bad time, but he's young and confident, and willing to take that risk.

They don't always have cake at Shoes, but they do today, and that's nice. Bo puts some candles in it and makes my dad blow them out. He acts like he's embarrassed, but he's not.

Then through the crowd of people emerges this woman with large eyelashes, large breasts, and extra-large hair. She carries a large, fishbowl-sized green drink with a big crazy straw in it. I assume it must be for me since people were always handing me big, colorful, crazy-looking things to play with. But she places it in front of my father and with a smoke-stained voice says, “This fruity one’s for the birthday boy.”

The table laughs.

My father says “Thanks, Tracy,” and acts like he’s embarrassed. But he’s not. He likes fruity drinks. Bo gives him a hard time for not drinking beer like the rest of this part of the country, but my dad has a sweet tooth. And as a 21-year-old, he doesn’t have a care in the world about blood sugar or diabetes or anything. It’s 1992 and everything's great.

The woman sets five more beers down on the table. She pulls them seemingly out of thin air.

Then, gesturing towards Bo, says, “This guy’s got the tab, right?”

Again, the table laughs.

Bo responds with a laughter-filled, “No no no…”

The woman leans down towards my mother, who’s holding me, and says in a hushed tone just loud enough for everyone to hear, “You got the good one, baby.”

My mother laughs. The whole table laughs.

The woman then bends down to my level, and says, “You take care of your momma, sweetie. She’s the only one you got.”

She then stands, looks at my father, says, “Happy birthday, baby!” and walks away. The crowd parts for her once again.

This woman, Tracy, within 45 seconds, charmed an entire party of people, including my mother, who is not the easiest charmee. She did this while simultaneously working through a large crowd of people, carrying 6 or more drinks, lightly insulting the masculinity of multiple people, and speaking kindly and generously to a baby and his young mother.

Tracy is the type of person who takes ownership and pride in whatever situation she finds herself in. Fortunately for this town, Tracy finds herself in the position of running a bar and restaurant that was opened by her father, Don, in the mid-70s. She worked there as a girl, paying her way through college, marriage, and a divorce. And here she is now, running the place, her two daughters, Meghan and Brianne, walking in her footsteps.

Her confidence and looks bring plenty of unwanted attention from a number of strange men that walk through the door. Legend has it, that she’s been proposed to over 200 times. And though she doesn’t need it, she has insulated herself with a number of very protective regulars who would do absolutely anything short of killing their own mother for her.

She does not forget a face. She may misplace a name but will find it by your second or third drink. She writes poetry on the side, just for her. She closes the restaurant for one week a year while giving all of her employees a full week’s pay. She cooks a big dinner and stays open until 11 pm on

Christmas Eve. Then everyone at the bar stumbles down the street for Christmas Eve midnight mass. She'd smoke anybody at horseshoes. She'd drink a man three times her size under the table. She'd check somebody's ego like a boxer, then pick them up, dust them off, and say, "It's OK, baby."

She is a hero.

Tracy is the type of person I want to grow up to be. And as much as I like Uncle Bo and Aunt Deb, sometimes I just wish my folks would leave me with Tracy at the bar. And if I wasn't 19 months old, I'd ask her to marry me, just like everyone else does.

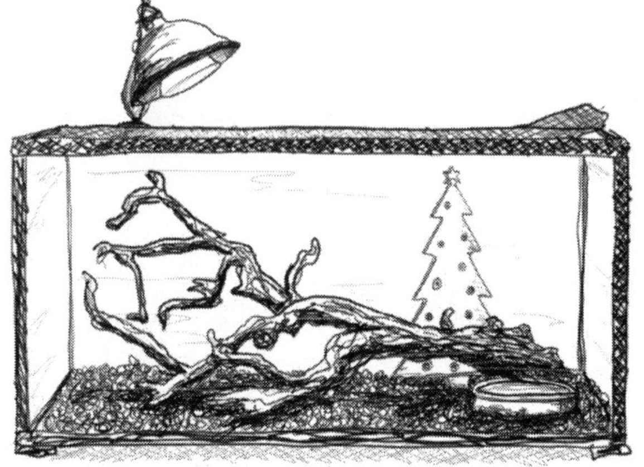

Uncle Rob

Now, talking about my Uncle Bo and Aunt Deb has me thinking about the other "Uncle" that is of no legal relation to me whatsoever.

Uncle Rob is my father's oldest friend.

As children, my dad and Rob lived down the street from one another. My dad was one of six and Rob, being an only child, would often frequent the house to play with my dad and his siblings. There are many a story of my young father and young Rob riding bikes to the park, taking parts out of parked cars, and generally having a real 70s time. You know, the good ol' days.

When Rob was about 10 years old, his father, a cartoon drawing of a Union man at a tire factory, passed away. Rob and his mother moved out of the house down the street from my grandparents and across town to live with Rob's mother's mother.

As an adult, this change in address would be no big deal. You'd see each other out and about, or you'd make a point to get across town every once in a while. But as a kid, riding your bike down the street and riding it across town are quite different things. Still, my grandmother is a saint if there ever was one, and she'd drive my dad out to Rob's grandma's house every once in a while. But imagine trying to do that with five other kids and all their nonsense going on, simultaneously.

At this point, my dad and Rob could've drifted apart. They'd still be friends, but the convenience factor (or lack thereof) naturally changes things.

But my dad, even as a child, is a very loyal and dedicated person—and set his mind on maintaining the friendship that he and Rob have had for all these years.

So, my father made a point of reaching out to Rob anytime the old neighborhood kids would get together. They'd play soccer or ride bikes or loiter in front of the convenience store. Whenever Rob was feeling down, my dad was the man he could talk to. My grandma would invite Rob and his mother over for holiday meals. Rob's mother would never take my grandmother up on the offer, but she always planned their own family meals to line up opposite my dad's family. That way, Rob could have two thanksgiving meals: lunch at home with his mom and grandma, then dinner with my dad, his siblings, and my grandparents.

But time moves on, and despite our intentions and our desire to hold onto the people we care about, peoples' boats float in different directions.

My dad joins the marching band.

Rob runs cross country.

My dad starts applying to colleges.

Rob drops out and starts cooking at Shoes.

Things happen.

But through all this, my dad makes a point to call Rob once every two weeks. Just to check in. Almost like they're pen pals. Their friendship starts to function that way too. Their phone calls turn into a combination of therapy session, confessional, and gossip column. And they continue this pattern for 40 years.

—

It's 1990-something. I am six years old and my brother is four, but quite mature for his age. We are in the back of a 1991 Oldsmobile Silhouette.

(My dad traded his LeBaron for this van when my mother got pregnant with my brother. He is a selfless man, but he loves his cars. The move to the minivan was a shift in his mindset, but not in his practice. I bet—even with two little bastards in the back, attempting to destroy the vehicle—it was the cleanest Oldsmobile Silhouette the world will ever know. He would take the Shop-Vac out to clean the floor mats every Saturday. He followed his floor mat cleaning with a trip to the same carwash that he used to go to in college. It was in what looked like an old Burger Shed. He knew the guy who *used* to run the place, and despite the fact that the new owner was an asshole, my father got sick pleasure from listening to this man go on and on about his delusional business ideas. On the way home from the carwash, my dad would cry laughing at how ridiculous and weird this guy was. I was six and even I understood the ridiculousness and irony of the over-ambitious, braggadocious carwash man.)

We're on our way to Rob's grandmother's house. Rob has recently moved back to town after a stint in Buffalo, New York, working with an improvisational modern dance troop—and he was staying at his grandma's house "until his next tour."

As a six-year-old, I don't really know or care about what Rob is doing or not doing, or whether his "next tour" is a fantasy or not. All I know for sure is that when we go to Uncle Rob's, my brother and I get to watch whatever movie we want, and we get to watch that movie with Rob's boa constrictor, Michael.

We had pets growing up, specifically dogs. The fate of the majority of these dogs was usually tragic. Pugs with heat strokes, French Bulldogs at the bottoms of swimming pools, various pound dogs and hound dogs that bit neighborhood kids and had to be put down, dogs that ended up living in metaphorical farms out in the country, and even some that went to live on real farms out in the country. I don't think me and my family were bad dog owners. I just think it's better that we don't keep dogs or look at dogs or interact with dogs or think about dogs—for the safety and longevity of the dogs. I love dogs. I don't care for indoor cats, but that's a personal preference. Outdoor cats are fine in a farm setting. But if they don't want to interact with me, I don't want to interact with them. It's better this way.

So, in the late nineties, other than when Jack Hannah would go on Late Night, we never got to see big ass snakes. *Unless* we went to go see Uncle Rob.

Rob's snake, Michael, was a fully grown female red-tailed boa constrictor. Rob said the snake was 7 feet, 4 inches long, and that my parents named me Michael because they liked her so much. Every time Rob would say this, my brother would laugh and my mother would look at me and shake her head, mouthing the words "He's joking" to me—as if I didn't get the joke or remember the last time he said it.

Rob fed the snake a live mouse every two weeks. She'd get an extra meal if we were coming over, just to upset my mother and get me and my brother jazzed. He said she was better behaved when she wasn't hungry. Rob made a point of exaggerating the way he said this to imply that if she *were* hungry, maybe she'd consider eating me and my brother as a substitution for her little mouse.

—

We park the van in the gravel drive of Rob's grandma's house and Rob's mother's dog, Ronda (a yippy little Yorkie-looking dog), greets us by jumping and jumping and scratching at my pregnant mother's legs.

"It's gonna be a girl!" calls Rob's mother, Cynthia, a lovely woman with absolutely no filter. "She only jumps at girls."

(I know this not to be true, as this stupid dog jumps at everything. She most recently broke her leg by barking and jumping at a reflection of herself in a floor mirror. The mirror fell on her, smashing her little leg. She wore a little doggy cast on it for a while, and still hobbles around on three legs, holding her injured leg up in the air. Not the way a dog would normally—holding it close to her body—But holding it straight out in an unnatural, almost tree branch-like position. Cynthia says that's just her trying to give me and my brother a high-five.)

My mother plays nice with the dog, trying to get it off her without kicking it, but eventually, my dad picks the dog up and hands it to Cynthia. "Glad to see Ronda has fully recovered after getting her cast off," he says.

"Oh yes...Ms. Ronda's just as friendly as ever," Cynthia says. "And she'd be the smartest dog in the world if she wasn't so stupid."

I think about that statement to this day. It's heavy stuff. I use variations of it on a daily basis:

"This weather'd be beautiful if it wasn't so crummy out."

"That would be such a pretty tree if they didn't chop it down."

"He could've been the oldest man in the world if he didn't throw himself in front of that bus 60 years ago."

The possibilities are endless. My wife hates it.

We stand in the front yard for a while. It's a pretty predictable neighborhood of mobile homes and manufactured housing that stays pretty well maintained. I've got a few friends that live in this neighborhood. There are a few houses with multiple cars parked in the front yard. The usual suspects are 70s Caprices, Cutlasses, and full-sized American vans. Usually, there is at least one donor vehicle being used for parts, and the other 1–2 cars float between running and almost running. As a kid, I love this, because you get to see the process of these vehicles coming together every time we go see Uncle Rob.

Eventually, we get into the house, and we're hit with what I now understand to be the smell of dog hair, laundry detergent, and marijuana. These smells have permeated the carpet and paneling of the house to the point where even today I'll be driving down the street, catch this same combination of smells coming from a rusted out, blue Dodge Neon, and be taken right back to Uncle Rob's house.

The dark-stained paneling and sponge green carpet are definitely original to the house. Come to think of it, the house was a bit of a time machine. The countertops. The linoleum. The fixtures in the bathroom. I loved it. As a child of the 90s, the aesthetic of the 1970s is so cool. All the weird colors. All the lines and shapes of the furniture. Everything is lower to the ground, which is dreamy for a kid. It allows you to be in control of your space as a smaller person (something that the giant sofas and sectionals of the late 80s/early 90s turned their backs on.)

I loved Uncle Rob's house. I suspect my parents were always a little concerned about the cleanliness of me and my brother sitting on bean bag chairs in some weird little room in some musky old trailer with some big old snake, but they never let on. And my brother and I couldn't care less about cleanliness. All we cared about is the fact that we were going to get to watch *The Mask* on VHS.

For those of you who don't know, *The Mask* is the second film in the Jim Carrey Trinity of 1994. The year began with *Ace Ventura: Pet Detective* — which is enough of a movie to make Jim Carrey a genius in the eyes of any ten-year-old boy, but to follow that masterpiece with *The Mask*— a zoot-suit-wearing, antihero-starring, paranormal-possession movie with a revenge plot, put Jim Carrey into a different class. The cherry on top of 1994, and Jim Carrey's ascension into permanent comedy royalty, was *Dumb and Dumber,* a movie that boys born between 1985 and 1993 can recite with Shakespearean precision.

Every time we go to Uncle Rob's, my brother and I spend 15–30 minutes perusing Rob's grandmother's collection of movies—a very impressive shelf full of mostly 80s action movies. She loves her some Sly Stallone, Arnold Schwarzenegger, and Bruce Willis. (His grandma, Cynthia's mother—who lives in and owns the house, though I'd never seen her—thought Bruce Willis looked like her late husband, who was also named Bruce.) Though the collection is extensive and quite impressive, my brother and I always get to watch whatever we want. And what do we want to watch? Again? For the fourth time in a row? *The Mask*.

So, my brother and I alert my parents to our movie of choice (I'm sure they already saw it coming) and we hunker down into our beanbag chairs.

Uncle Rob enters, mouse in hand. This mouse knows not yet his fate. Rob goes off on his typical, "Do one of you boys want to feed Michael? She gets awfully temperamental when she hasn't eaten." He takes the blanket off of the terrarium.

Usually, this big reveal shows us a heat lamp, a large glass tank complete with very realistic imitation rainforest sticks so the snake feels right at home, and of course, Michael, the big ass boa constrictor.

Occasionally Rob would change up the sticks. You know, give Michael a sense of variety. He'd decorate for Christmas, St Patty's, and whatever other holiday struck his fancy. I'm sure Michael really appreciated the effort.

So, despite the Valentine's Day decorations on Michael's tank this time around, there was one glaring change up in the typical show.

The absence of one very large snake.

My four-year-old brother lets out a strong, "Uh-oh..." followed by a look that my pregnant mother gives my father. A look that can only be translated as "You've got to be fucking kidding me." (An appropriate response given a missing 7ft snake.)

Uncle Rob attempts to keep my parents from panicking but instead lets out the word, "Huh..." (An appropriate response if you're confused but not worried about the whereabouts of a 7ft snake. And an absolutely garbage response if you're trying to keep a pregnant lady from freaking out about a missing 7ft snake.)

My mother again looks at my father, then back at Rob, then at both me and my brother, and says, "Hey boys...I know we were going to have some cake after dinner but why don't we just pick up some sandwiches and ice cream on the way home. Dad's going to stay here and help Uncle Rob look for his snake."

At this point, I ask, "But don't they need our help?"

To which my mother replies by saying the exact same thing she just said, but louder and with more intensity in her eyes. "WHY DON'T WE JUST PICK UP SOME SANDWICHES AND ICE CREAM ON THE WAY HOME. DAD'S GOING TO STAY HERE AND HELP UNCLE ROB LOOK FOR HIS SNAKE."

We understood.

As my mother, brother, and I wave our goodbyes from the van, Uncle Rob, Ms. Cynthia, and my father (whom Rob will drive home on his motorcycle after they find Michael) stand on the front porch.

At this point, I feel like something is a little off. It's not the absence of my father in the car. It's not the absence of the snake. It's not the absence of Rob's grandma—I'd never seen her. It's not that we didn't get to watch our movie.

I can't place it.

But as I sit at the kitchen table, across from my brother, eating the shredded chicken sandwiches and ice cream sundaes that we picked up on the way home, I am overcome with a sense of dread—the first time I've felt this emotion.

I realize what was missing from our typical goodbyes at Uncle Rob's—the presence of one very small, very yippy dog named, Ronda.

I hear Rob's motorcycle pull into our driveway around 9:30 that night. We sneak halfway down the steps to listen to my parents' conversation, something we did fairly regularly.

Rob and my parents talk for a bit. We can't quite get a read on whether or not they found the snake, but Rob leaves, so my brother and I decide to save our recap for the morning.

At breakfast the next day, we sit eating our cereal (Cinnamon Crunchy Squares, a Cinnamon Toast Crunch knockoff), waiting for our parents to come downstairs. My father shows first, moving quickly, on his way out the door, heading to work. My brother comes in hot with the questions.

"Hey, Dad! How's Rob? How's the snake? You find the snake?"

"Everything's fine. Love you guys! See you in a bit," he responds, totally avoiding the questions and walking out the door.

"Dammit," says my brother. "How'd he just brush them questions off?"

"He's a master, dude. You came in too hot with the questions. You gotta tighten up. Let me handle it with Mom," I say as I hear her coming down the stairs.

"Good morning, Mom! How'd ya sleep?" I ask, like a real brownnoser.

"Fine, thank you. Look at you guys making your own breakfast! Big boys!"

"Yeah…Hey mom…they uh…ever find that snake?" I ask as she pours her coffee.

"I'm sure the snake is fine." (The most motherly version of "No, they didn't find her. Won't you shut up about the damn snake.")

"Real subtle," my brother mumbles to me.

"And how about the dog, Ronda? They ever find her?"

At this point, my mother realizes that we've put two and two together and without turning around from the coffee machine, she pauses, then says,

"I'm sure Ronda is fine."

At that point, I look at my brother as we both realize that we'd never see that stupid little dog again. We also recognize all the other dogs that we've known—whose lives also ended in tragic circumstances. We take that in, and my mother recognizes our pause. She tries to find the necessary words for talking to children about a boa constrictor eating a dog, but before she can come up with something, my brother exclaims,

"Another one bites the dust."

TOMMYLAND
CARWASH
Acrobics by Tammie
COM NG
SOON

Tommy and Tammie

Tommy and Tammie Thompson are the proprietors of Toledo's premier suburban-style aerobic studio/car wash.

"Why does something like that exist?" you may ask.

Well...

Tommy's dad, Big Tom Thompson of Thompson Builders and Development, built a series of strip malls in the early 90s.

After getting their real estate licenses revoked and going to prison, Tommy and his wife Tammie decided to get in on the family business. And by "get in on the family business" I mean that when Tommy's mother, Brenda, and Big Tom got divorced, Brenda ended up with the shopping plaza on the corner of Central Ave and MLK and gave all managing rights of said plaza to Tommy and Tammie, just to spite Big Tom.

Big Tom knew that his son, Tommy, was...well...Tommy is an idiot.

His whole situation in those days wasn't far from the 1994 film *Tommy Boy*, starring Chris Farley. The physical resemblance is uncanny and the level of idiocracy isn't far off. So, when the movie came out, it didn't take long for people to start making comments. The comments got so out of hand that Tommy began to build up a world in his head where he was a well-respected, well-spoken businessman with all sorts of good things going on. He started carving little figurines on the back deck of his house (maybe his only real skill) and physically building his ideal world on a ping pong table in his basement. He called it "Tommyland!" He was a real visionary, and declared this often, randomly, to himself.[4]

As I type this out, I realize that Tommyland, and maybe Tommy himself, seem sad. As I read that last paragraph back, I feel for Tommy. I empathize with him. I think,

"Maybe under different circumstances..."

"Maybe Tommy has unspoken potential..."

I think, "You got this Tommy! Don't let those people bully you. Tommyland *can* be your reality!"

But that's my overly optimistic Midwestern millennial mindset showing.

That's the "if you work hard enough in this world, you can do anything" garbage that they used to teach us in the 90s.

But if I'm going to be realistic here...

If I'm going to be honest...

---

[4] Despite it being an equally eccentric piece of work, Tommy Thompson's "Tommyland" is not a reference to the Tommy Lee memoir, *Tommyland.* When questioned about it at a later date, Tommy Thompson will happily tell anyone, without doubt or a sense of exaggeration, that Tommy Lee stole the title of the book from *him* and based some of the stories in the memoir on pieces of Tommy Thompson's own life.

Tommy is a bad guy. He's not Chris Farley's character in the movie. This guy forges checks from people's dead grandparents. This guy steals lumber off construction sites and hangs around long enough to shit in the Porta Johns. This guy eats grapes while he walks around the grocery just to leave the empty grape stems sitting on some random shelf next to the potato chips. This guy definitely leans his seat back on an airplane.

So, don't feel bad for Tommy.

On top of his traditionally slimy behavior, Tommy will occasionally take his Tommyland fantasies into the real world.

He'll talk about his "businesses" and his "portfolios." He'll throw around vocabulary that the real Tommy has barely even heard before. He speaks so confidently in this state that people who have never met him before are impressed. And people who have only met him a few times before may second guess themselves on their preconceptions of Tommy Thompson.

He's gotten loans this way. He's gotten investors this way. He's been charged with fraud this way. He's represented himself in court this way.

Don't feel bad for Tommy.

…

Now, Tammie's a different story.

I'm just kidding. She may be worse than Tommy.

Tammie is the fifth of six sisters: Tiffany, Tina, Tonya, Trisha, Tammie, and Tommie. Tammie's twin sister, Tommie (not to be confused with her husband, Tommy), would say that they're both the fifth sister. But Tammie's the type to *really* emphasize the fact that she was born three minutes before. She'll tell you that she's fifth even though her sister, Tommie, says they're both fifth, despite the fact that you're just meeting her for the first time and you have no reason to know or care about her or her sister.

She's loose like that with all sorts of information, but never anything useful. She could monologue at a brick wall, then be flabbergasted that the wall didn't respond positively to what she had to say. I've seen her make eyes at a mannequin in the suiting section of the department store before. She's the type to be aroused by furniture, or vehicles, or vegetables. She loves monogrammed bags and animal print shoes and bitching to her new hairdresser about her old hairdresser.

She's had the same hairdresser for 27 years. Connie. You know Connie. She's the best.

But Tammie's a freak.

And despite all her wildly specific characteristics, I could drive up I-75 right now, throw a handful of peanut shells out the window between Lima and Toledo and I'll probably hit at least nine Tammies. Tammies are everywhere.

But our particular Tammie is special. Our Tammie, Tammie Thompson, has a photographic memory.

Now, I'm sure when you talk to the Tammies in your life, they tell you crazy stuff like this, too. And you blow it off because she's wild and it doesn't matter.

The first time I heard about this photographic memory, I thought the same thing. "Classic Tammie. Telling us she's the real fifth sister even though her twin sister says they're both fifth and she saw this hot guy at the store who was actually a mannequin and she's got a photographic memory and her last hairdresser was so crazy…blah blah blah."

But Tammie Thompson has an honest-to-goodness photographic memory. The only reason it hasn't gotten her into trouble is that people don't take anything she says seriously. And rightfully so. Like I said, she's a freak.

But with a memory like hers, she could really do something in this world. She could be a spy. She could be a code breaker. Hell, she could hang around Toledo and work at Channel 4. They'd be better off paying her to drink white wine and shit talk, rather than do any real investigative reporting.

While I imagine her memory could be used for good, the only thing Tammie Thompson's memory is known for is the Toledo Tech Fizzle of 1998.

In the thick of the dot-com bubble and the height of America Online, Tammie and Tommy (her husband, not Tammie's sister, Tommie) Thompson decided that they, along with everybody else, should get in on some of this freshly harvested internet. And while most normal people looking to get in on the action just bought stock in some tech companies, hoping they could ride those dial-up coattails to the top, the Thompsons wanted more. So, with the confidence of Tommy's Tommyland-style alter-ego, his father's real estate holdings, and Tammie's ability to recall any information she'd ever seen, Tammie and Tommy made an outrageous amount of phone calls, forged an amazing amount of documentation, and brought on a wild number of legitimate investors in an attempt to put Toledo on the map as THE tech capital of North America.

I know what you're thinking. How could a person convince any logical and sane person that Toledo, Ohio is the future of innovation and technology? Not Silicon Valley, but Toledo, Ohio?

And I'm with you. It seems dumb. But that's exactly what the Thompsons did.

They started 50 or more websites for companies that didn't really exist. I mean, they existed. But they were all just Tammie and Tommy. They forged Tommy's father's name (not a hard thing to do when you have the same name as your dad) and posed as him on multiple occasions. They took out loans in his name. They took out mortgages in his name. They made construction and renovation deals with start-ups and manufacturing companies on behalf of Thompson Construction and Development (or rather, Toledo Technology Development: a TC&D Company).

And yes—your average criminal or even advanced ID theft co-op would run themselves ragged trying to keep up with this level of fraud. But the Thompsons were no average criminal operation.

Tommy was the type to trip himself up at the first obstacle, but his confidence and delusion on the front end were perfect. He believed every word that came out of his own mouth.

And once that first obstacle showed up, there was Tammie in all her glory. She remembered every last detail of every conversation and transaction. She knew secretaries' names. She knew the names of bank managers' kids. She could talk about boats with CEOs. She could pretend to be looking at a spreadsheet and pull accurate numbers out of thin air. She had alter egos and would do different voices for each character. She used her sisters' names as monikers for every secretary, middle manager, and recruiter of Toledo Technology Development: a TC&D Company.

Now, eventually, something has to break the camel's back in a story like this. Maybe bank statements aren't adding up. Maybe construction keeps getting delayed. Maybe someone skips town and travels all over the world forging passports and medical licenses and cool stuff like that.

But no, not here. This is way stupider. The eventual tell for our friends at Toledo Technology Development is the fact that Tammie, even when acting as one of her alter-egos, can't *not* talk about the fact that "she's the real fifth sister and her twin sister says they're both fifth but she knows she's the real fifth because she's just a little older."

Tammie, with all of her brilliance, with all of her gumption, with her ability to keep everything else straight, can't seem to understand that a stupid and irrelevant piece of information when repeated multiple times during the same phone call by supposedly different people is the biggest, strangest, dumbest red flag you could throw up.

I know that may be hard to follow, so here's an example of a conversation between Tammie, Tonya [Tammie], Tiffany [also Tammie], and an investor—let's call him Ronnie.

Tammie: Good morning Mr. McArthur. This is Tammie at TTD. I work with Tommy Thompson. We spoke the other day regarding our new project. Is this still a good time for you? I know you're very busy but Mr. Thompson was so excited to hear that you're looking to get involved.

Ronnie: Good morning, Tammie. Great to hear from you. I spoke with your secretary, Tina, the other day, and she said I should expect your call. It sounds like you have a really solid group out there.

Tammie: I'd like to think we do. It's a fun group, but we pride ourselves on getting things done. That's why we try to incorporate our construction and development teams so early. They've got some progressive ideas regarding open office space. These are exciting times and we think our work spaces should reflect that.

Ronnie: Sounds great! I'd love to get out there and have a look sometime soon. The renderings you sent over look incredible.

Tammie: We'd love to have you. The lakefront project is gorgeous. And if you've never been to the

Great Lakes, may I say, they're called "Great" for a reason.

Ronnie: (light laughter)

Tammie: Mr. McArthur...

Ronnie: Please, call me Ronnie. Mr. McArthur is my father.

Tammie: (light laughter) You got it, Ronnie! Hey, I've got to get on a plane right now, but I just got a notice that Tiffany, our lab head is online. Do you mind if I transfer you over so she can introduce herself and run you through the rest of our onboarding process?

Ronnie: No problem. You can do all of that from the airport? You can see if she's online and transfer me through from the *airport*?

Tammie: (light laughter) We sure can. This is the future, Mr. McArthur. And we're glad you're going to be a part of it. Good talking with you. Hopping on this plane to go see my sister for the weekend. Twin sister, actually. Though we're twins, I'm technically older than she is. I've got four older sisters and technically she has five older sisters, and though she would say we're both fifth, I think we all know that I'm the real fifth sister.

Ronnie: (Nervous laughter) Well...have a nice trip.

Tammie: Thanks! I'll transfer you.

Tiffany: Hello Mr. McArthur. This is Tiffany [Tammie] Taylor. How are you doing today?

Ronnie: I'm doing great! How are you?

Tiffany: I'm doing great! Thanks for asking. Is this a good time for you? Tammie says you're quite busy and I'd like to respect your time.

Ronnie: This is great. Go right ahead.

Tiffany: Perfect. I know we're on the phone now, and that's all well and good, But I feel we'd be more efficient working electronically. We do a lot of email correspondence. Do you work with email already?

Ronnie: Somewhat. But we still work with a lot of paper—faxes and whatnot. I'm pretty comfortable with email, but I'm always available via phone.

Tiffany: That's great. I'm sure you'll be quite comfortable with email in no time at all. After all, you're in the technology industry now. And I can guarantee, Mr. McArthur, that you're working with the best. Toledo is the future...Mr. McArthur, I'm so sorry to have to do this. But I'm getting another call.

Ronnie: Is everything all right?

Tiffany: Yes. I hate to do this, but it's my baby sister. Strange that she'd call me at work. It must be an emergency.

Ronnie: I completely understand.

Tiffany: I mean...I'm sure everything's fine. She's my twin sister actually. She's still my baby sister though. As I am the fifth of six sisters. And she's technically the sixth. She says we're both fifth, but everyone knows I'm the real fifth sister since I came out first.

I'll put you through to my secretary, Tonya. She'll get your TTD email set up and get your account info sent over. Again, I'm so sorry. We'll talk soon.

...

The call may go on like this for another 15 minutes, with Tammie impersonating various fictional employees whom all happen to have twin sisters that they bring up in conversation for no reason whatsoever.

Shocking stuff.

After a phone call like this, I assume our friend, Ronnie, probably assumes that whatever weird prescription drugs he's been abusing are hitting a little hard because there's no way that all three of those ladies are the fifth of six sisters and would talk openly about their twin sister on the same phone call with a total stranger. That would be crazy.

But that's exactly what happened with hundreds of investors all across North America. For two and a half years, Tammie threw in weird little details about her twin sister while talking to hundreds of investors, bankers, and anyone else who would listen. It wasn't until those investors' and bankers' paths started to cross that anyone picked up on the fact that the odds of everyone who works at Toledo Technology Development having a twin sister that they can't stop talking about is pretty low.

After this flag goes up. It doesn't take long for the feds to take notice of the Thompsons' business dealings.

A few calls to Big Tom as well as Tammie's sisters (who know every detail because Tammie can't keep a secret) and the federal government has an open-and-shut case regarding Toledo Technology Development.

Tommy and Tammie both serve almost identical sentences of three years in federal prison. Tammie gets out a little early for accidentally giving up valuable information on a few of the shadier investors—the kind of people the feds actually care about. And Tommy gets out a touch late, waiting for his fictional lawyer to file some paperwork.

By the time they get out, Y2K has come and gone, the Twin Towers no longer exist, and as it turns out the internet was just a fad. But for the Thompsons, it's like the 90s never ended.

They almost instantly get pregnant with twin boys, Travis and Tyler. (Both of whom later wait tables in tandem at Olive Garden, then go on to "practice law" in Columbus. Not as "lawyers," but as some strange sort of "advisors" at a "law" office. Scamming is hereditary sometimes.)

Tommy and Tammie are then (thanks to the divorce of Big Tom and Brenda) handed the keys to the shopping plaza at Central Ave and MLK. You know, the one with the old Burger Shed in the parking lot. The Burger Shed had been turned into a carwash in the 80s, but Tommy liked carwashes, so Tommy boots the tenant and decides to run the carwash his way—like a big weirdo. And despite the fact that there are two vacant spaces in the building, Tammie likes the storefront that's closest to the street and she removes the only veterinary clinic in the area—replacing it with her very own aerobics studio, Aerobics by Tammie. (She started attending aerobics classes while in prison and really fell in love with it. It's seemingly her true passion. She probably loves it more than her kids. Again, it's like 1995, but forever.)

—

And all these details come rushing back, though I can't understand why my brain would store nonsense like this, long-term. But here I am. Present day. Standing in the snow in the middle of the night. At the corner of Central Ave and MLK in beautiful majestic Toledo Ohio, looking at a carwash in the parking lot of a shopping center. The storefronts are dark because it's the middle of the night, but the yellow glow of the vinyl marquee that sits by the street illuminates the snow.

The two sign spaces closest to the ground say

COM NG

and

SOON

The sign above that reads,

Aerobics by Tammie

Above that, just the word,

CARWASH

And above that, in bright red plastic letters popping out of a thin yellow sign,

TOMMYLAND

because time travel does exist and dreams do come true.

Part Two:

...

Narrative Theory on Northwest Ohio

in the style of

Undereducated First Person Stream of Consciousness

A Warm Welcome Home

The reason I'm standing in the parking lot of the Tommyland Carwash in the middle of the night is that this is where the tire of my rental car (a slightly used but completely smoked out Honda Civic) happened to snag a 3-inch deck screw on the way home from the Detroit Metropolitan Wayne County Airport.

My folks live about 40 minutes south of Tommyland, in a completely different town, but I had a hankering for some regional fare on the way home and decided to make a detour through beautiful, majestic downtown Toledo. But instead of getting my coney dog, I get a flat tire in the snow.

Despite the unfortunate nature of the flat tire, I must add that I'm pretty impressed with the rental car people. Within the hour, they roll up with a tow truck and a Jeep as a replacement car. Sure, they could've just patched the tire, but I'm thrilled to see the Jeep as I didn't expect the snow in April. On top of that, we are in America's Motor City. There's a sad irony in picking up a little Honda in a town built on American manufacturing. (Not that I have anything against Japanese automobiles. Great cars! I own a Prius. And everybody roasts me for it. But that fuel economy…unreal.)

So, despite the timeless 16mpg of the Jeep, I'm grateful for it, as I pull into my parents' driveway at 2 am. I called ahead and told them not to wait up, but as I walk in the door I see my father get up off the couch. He has attempted to wait up by watching some Ken Burns docuseries on the National

Parks, but let's be honest, that plan was doomed from the start. If they could package Ken Burns's voice in a pill, they'd put Benadryl and NyQuil out of business.

He greets me with a sleepy "Welcome home, Bubba," and a big bear hug. We come from a long line of big bear huggers on my father's side of the family—beautifully stocky, corn-fed Catholic people whose roots trace back to a long line of German candy makers. If we follow that lineage back far enough, I imagine Santa Clause himself to be a great-great-grandpa somewhere in the mix.

My father heads to bed as I romp up the stairs to my childhood bedroom. Though my bed is still there, it seems my brother has turned this room into a home gym, complete with bench press, treadmill, and stationary bicycle. The room isn't all that big—maybe 10ft by 10ft—and while I am pretty impressed with the use of space, I know, with almost certainty, that I will break one of my toes on a kettlebell before the weekend is through.

I drift off to sleep and before I know it, I awake to the sound of clanking metal and the intro to Bell Biv DeVoe's "Poison." (Brother only lifts to new jack swing. A real nightmare, but absolute gold if you're trying to write something like this.) I open my eyes and there's my brother, doing squats just inches from my sleeping head.

"Hey man! Welcome home! Any way I could get a spot?" he asks.

Now to clarify, my brother is not a meathead. He's not really the gym rat type. He's a 6-foot-tall vegan with hair and a beard down to his waist. His weight and physique fluctuate like that of an overzealous Oscar-hungry method actor—

meaning he could drop or put on 50 lbs in a matter of six weeks, without even thinking about it.

He's kidding about the "spot." He's currently in a phase where he's doing more reps rather than maxing out his potential "GAINS." His former routine involved moving around a *lot* of weight. And honestly, our people are built for moving around a lot of weight. But this weight room of his (my childhood bedroom) is above the garage, and after talking with my brother for two minutes, it seems moving this amount of weight around caused an "issue" with one or two of the floor joists (the joists that keep this garage attic/bedroom/weight room from crashing down on my father's comically clean cars that sleep below). Evidently, while my brother was moving some metal around the other day, these joists made a "weird sound." The sound was "weird" enough that my brother decided to change up his workout routine—not enough to move the routine to a more reasonable location (Basement, maybe, or ground level at the very least) but any sort of adjustment or ability to improvise is a big step for my brother—possibly the most routine based person I know (strange though his routines may be.)

"I heard about Fish, man. So sorry my dude. Tragic," he says, laughing while transferring into some sort of lunge-squat.

"Oh, yes! Thanks, man. Brutal stuff. I can't wait for the funeral. It's going to be outrageous," I respond.

"How's everybody taking it?" he asks. "Does everybody know?"

“They’re taking it as well as they can, I guess. Dave’s coming in this morning and heading straight to the wake. Everyone else got in last night.”

“Damn. That’s too much,” he responds. “Funeral’s tomorrow?”

“Today, dude. Wake’s at 10. Funeral’s sometime this afternoon, I guess. We’d love to see you there.”

“Jesus. At St. Pat’s?”

“Nope. Driving up to Port Clinton after the wake.”

“Fuck off. Waterfront funeral?”

“Yeah…Put-in-Bay,” I reply.

“No way! You’re putting the coffin on the ferry?”

“Yeah, man,” I say, nodding my head. “It’s what he would’ve wanted.”

“You guys are sick,” he says, shaking his head. “This has gotta be expensive.”

“It’s what he would’ve wanted,” I reply.

He laughs. “That’s messed up.”

“Well…‘A celebration of life is a *celebration* of life.’”

He finishes up his reps and we both go downstairs to meet my parents. They're both off of work today. It's a fairly cold, yet sunny, Friday in April. It flurried last night, but the rest of the winter snow has been melting for the past couple of weeks.

Usually, at this point in the year, there are still big grey and brown piles of snow sitting around town. The roads are usually pretty clear and the mounds of snow, salt, and grit that have been accumulating since Thanksgiving have turned to slightly smaller mounds of snow, salt, and grit, surrounded by a mixture of green and brown grass. But because of the flurries last night, the gritty, end-of-season ice mounds (along with the grass and driveways) are covered with a nice inch of fresh snow.

I happen to love the snow. (I didn't love it last night when I got the flat tire, but I've moved on.) It's a nice welcome home present. We haven't gotten any snow in Tennessee over the past few years, and it feels like a baptism of sorts.

My father, on the other hand, hates the snow this late in the year. Truth be told, he may hate any snow that happens after the start of the new year. He was born in a town east of here. He was raised in this town. He has raised his kids in this town. He has seen the snow, and he is over it. His long-term goals involve ending up in Florida, or maybe on a beach in Portugal. Portugal sounds nice. His short-term goals involve trying to shovel this snow off the driveway before God and the sun melt it themselves (probably by 10 am.) If it were me, I'd wait until 10 and let the sun do the work. But my father knows better. He knows not to trust the sun. The sun is an unfamiliar friend in this part of the country, and though it is welcome when it comes, it doesn't stay long, so you must shovel the snow yourself. And once my brother and I see my dad out there at 6:30 in the morning, shoveling by himself, we look at each other, roll our eyes and get out there with him. This brings my father nothing but joy, despite the fact that neither my brother nor I have even close to the level of meticulousness that my dad applies to shoveling, landscaping, and keeping cars.

But the driveway gets finished. As the sun begins to melt the snow that we've moved, my brother and I get some quality time with my dad and for just a moment, despite the craziness that happens all around us on a daily basis, all is right with the world.

We get back inside and my mother is brewing coffee.

"Good morning, Michael!" she says, giving me my first hug of the day. (Lots of hugs at home. The whole family is big on hugs when we greet, hugs when we leave, and hugs in between, increased exponentially with alcohol consumption.)

My mother, like my father, is also a lovely person. She comes from a line of people whose origins are most likely Scotch-Irish via Smokey Mountains, though if you ask my grandpa (her father) where we come from, he'll take a sip of his beer, pause, say the word, "Detroit," pause again (while his entire life flashes before his eyes), then take another sip. Though they're not as "huggy" as my dad's people, the presence of my father and his people has certainly rubbed off on them.

Unlike many of her peers, my mother is constantly questioning and reinventing herself and what she thinks of the world around her—not in big dramatic ways, but in little, gradual changes. Despite the occasional large change (eating habits perhaps), she seems to push through these changes without really rocking the family boat. The crucial part of keeping this boat afloat is the willingness of my siblings and my father to just go with the flow despite the occasional storm-level changeup in my mother's ideologies. (One year they all decided, under the direction of my mother and a couple of documentaries, to go vegan right before Thanksgiving. I was furious.)

The group veganism has since subsided, but my brother still holds tight to his animal-free eating habits. And while on the surface this seems healthy, his vegan habits come with a lot of sugar, caffeine, and processed food consumption. I think this is what pushed my mother and the rest of the family past their initial vegan kick and into a more holistic way of eating.

But where my mother can adjust and refine her relationship with the world, my brother takes every experience he has, places it deep within his soul, and lets it become a part of his ethos. This is what has allowed him to become the long-haired, dandelion-eating, Faygo-Red-Pop-drinking, nocturnal, vegan bodybuilder that he is today.

So, the four of us, my mom, dad, brother, and I, sit down for a morning cup of coffee—a nice adult moment that I take for granted on the daily. But having this moment at the kitchen table of my childhood home feels like a treat. A bit of a time warp. But the best version of a time warp.

In fact, the whole house is kind of a time machine unto itself. It's easy to say this about my grandparents' house or Uncle Rob's Grandma's trailer—with all the paneling and carpet—it's all aesthetics, but with a childhood home, it's weirder. It's not furnishings or decor or anything. It's memories. It's not wallpaper as much as it is the smell of the furnace. It's the fact that my mother still buys the same brand of coffee and still keeps it in the same cabinet. And though my parents share decorating habits with a lot of other people in this part of the country, they have a very particular way that they do things and you don't realize that you miss those weird little things until you come back home after being gone for a while.

But while we're on the subject of decor, I'd like to take some time out of our scheduled programming to discuss the domestic aesthetic choices of Northwest Ohio.

—

As a resident of Northwest Ohio, there are a few camps of decorating into which you can fall.

If you live in a newer suburban home (built after 1980), your decor can be described as...

1. *These Are My Things*: This style of decor involves placing random things that you own around your house. These could be things that you acquire over time or things that you purchase all at once because you "need to decorate." The later variation, who decorate all at once, can either buy their things at stores that specialize in general home decor or at craft stores that also sell home decor.[5] A home decorated in this style generally revolves around the seasons while constant decorations remain. Those

---

[5] "Hello...young man...where do you guys keep all your pumpkins? I saw the ad in the paper that said you were having a sale on pumpkins cus you're making room for Christmas stuff but I'm afraid that someone came in here and bought up all the pumpkins before I even got the chance because I'm not seeing any pumpkins anywhere..."

constants may include but are not limited to: ceramic frogs, full-size replicas of medieval armor, framed posters from old movies, garland, metal signs that say the word "GATHER" on them, DVD collections, CD towers, large couches, large televisions, local artisan pottery, and family photos/photos of dad's band with the bass player from Three Dog Night.

2. *Suburban Hunting Lodge*: Gatlinburg, TN, is a *formerly* quiet town at the foot of the Smokey Mountains. Over the past half-century, it has slowly turned into a tourism Mecca. The pancake houses and lodge-style motels that used to sit decorated for Christmas, looking up at the majesty of the country's oldest mountain range, now sit surrounded by billboards letting people know that the state's largest upside-down hotel is just 3 miles down the road. If you choose to drive to this upside-down hotel, you'll pass four "As Seen On TV" stores (for seeing products that are normally exclusively sold on *TELEVISION*, but in *REAL LIFE!)* a giant roadside shark (for just $15, you too can take a photo of your family in the mouth of said shark), about 30 different go-kart tracks, 130 different airbrush t-shirt shops (that also sell bongs, medieval weapons, or both), and 500,000 wooden statues of black bears in 1000 different parking lots surrounded by hundreds of fleece blankets with wolves on them.

If you've ever been lucky enough to find yourself in one of these wooden-bear-filled parking lots, you know that the human mind is no match for the glory that is a wooden bear, carved by a chainsaw, covered in polyurethane, that is designed to hold a roll of toilet paper. And now that this wooden toilet paper bear is in your possession, you know that it is a part of who you are. It is your identity. And you must fill your entire home with shiny wooden objects. Your lampshade must have a moose on it. Your rugs must look like the skin of animals. (Sure, you can put that rug on top of the carpet. It's fine.) There must be a framed print of a Native American man (who is somehow also a wolf) standing on a rock looking at the stars above your bed. You must get more polyurethane-covered wooden animals for around the house. You must have little stuffed black bears around the house. This is who you are. This is your home. And you're always in Gatlinburg, even when you're not.

3. *I Love the Beach*: This genre of home decor is not specific to Northwest Ohio. But this area of the country is PRIME for seafaring fantasies due to its far-but-not-too-far distance to the Atlantic Ocean and its very close proximity to Lake Erie.

   While Lake Erie is lovely, the grey color of the sky, the brown tint to the water, the quantity of mayflies, and the nuclear power plants that interrupt the otherwise ocean-esque sunsets leave a "close but no cigar" feeling buried deep within anyone who grew up near this third coast. (I should also note that I, along with any other person who grew up and spent time near the Lake Erie coast, will defend the integrity of her beautiful waters until the police pull us off your slanderous body. How dare you come in here, to this bar, and talk bad about Mother Erie! Go back to Lake Michigan, you blue-blooded, clear-watered, wooden sailboat piece of shit! And say "hi" to your mother for me!)

   This *beachy* style decor involves pastel paint choices, seashell soaps, starfish lamps, and seahorse towels.

> Furniture choices may also be dictated by this Fire Island fantasy, making wicker and linen-colored couches a must. Feel free to put that photo of you and David in Hilton Head on your nightstand. Feel free to put that retextured, printed canvas of that random beach on your wall. Sure, you bought it at Target, but you deserve that reminder of all the good times. Blue skies, blue waters. Some beach, somewhere. You and your kids and David. On vacation. That's happiness.
>
> But until you get there again, you have this Jimmy Buffet Margarita Machine, this electric fan on your back deck, and this visor that you bought at some shop in Sanibel. And that will work just fine.

Now, if you live in an older home, maybe a turn-of-the-century Victorian situation in the older part of town, you may decorate in one of the former styles, though the lovely details of your house may prevent you from going ALL-IN with a theme the way people do in the suburbs. But odds are the architecture of the house and the piano that came with it will lean you towards antiques in your decorating decisions.

This path of antiquities can lean you towards something people would consider "good taste," or if you don't believe in that sort of thing, you can enter a domain that can only be described as "gaudy as hell." (As a kid, I loved going into houses like this. The level of maximalism is something that I didn't grow up with, but seeing the choices that people make when money is no object and style inspiration comes from a more animalistic, "Oh look, so shiny!" sort of place was a real treat.

Now, of course, any and all of the above styles may be mixed together—but that just becomes a more eclectic version of "*These Are My Things.*" And let's be honest, everyone's decorating style, when you really get down to it, is just a different version of *"These Are My Things."* Even people who read books about mindfulness and decide that they're *minimalists,* all of the sudden, decorate with the minimal amount of things that they still have.[6]

Some people like beachy things. Some people like wooden bear statues. Some people like Scandinavian inspired spindly little dowel legs on short little overpriced, uncomfortable sofas. But beauty's in the eye of the beholder, I guess, and I'll tell you right now, I'd take a nap in one of those giant Midwestern recliners over some city slicking, mid-century modern teak framed yada yada any day! So poke fun all you want at my aunt's seashell towels, she'll have the last laugh: as you're commuting on the train back to your minimalism-inspired four-story walk-up, she's watching *Wheel of Fortune* from her huge-ass reclining sectional.

—

As my mother scoops out the beans for our second pot of coffee (with a seashell-shaped coffee scoop), she probes with the smallest questions as only a mother can.

---

[6] Listen, Jeromy, I know you left that book out on your coffee table, just so. You wanted me to see it. You wanted me to think you're deep. I know you're not deep, Jeromy. And why are you trying to impress me? I'm not your Tinder date, Jeromy. I'm just delivering your pizza.

“So, what’s the agenda for this weekend?”

My dad laughs.

“What?” she asks. “I want the *scoop*,” she says as she scoops another spoonful of coffee grounds.

“Well…the wake is here in a couple hours, and the funeral’s this afternoon,” I say.

“Dave gets in this morning,” my brother adds.

“YOU GUYS!” my mother half exclaims. “What’s Dave doing these days? He still live out west with that girl? He still dumb?”

I laugh. “Yes. Same ol’.”

“You guys are messed up. I can’t believe all of you’ve kept up all these years. Is he happy out there? His friend seems nice.”

“His *friend!”* my brother says, laughing. “Why is everyone someone’s *‘friend’* until they get married?”

“They’re engaged, Mom,” I say.

“Oh, that’s right,” she says. (She didn’t forget that he was getting married. She’s just hamming it up.) “You guys are getting so old! I’m just losing track of time.” (No, she’s not.) “Does he still think your sister is a little bastard child?”

We all laugh. “No. I think we blew that one a few years ago,” I say.

[I must explain. A few years after graduating high school, some fifteen years ago, Dave and our friend, Johnny Waterbottle, were driving over to my parent's house to pick me up.[7] [8]

My sister, who is 8 years younger than us, came up in conversation because Dave, innocently and naively (though stupidly enough), decided to ask a simple question regarding my then 12-year-old sister. And our friend, Mr. Waterbottle, decided to take advantage of such an opportunity.]

The question, posed by Dave, was,

"Hey, J, who's that girl who's always hanging out at Mic's house?"

Johnny Waterbottle replies, "That's Mic's sister."

At this point, a normal person would pause, and either put two and two together or ask a follow-up question. But not Dave. Dave went with, "No…I know who Mic's sister is. But

---

[7] Probably around Thanksgiving or something. Around the holidays, twenty-somethings who have moved away from home for school or whatever, *love* meeting up and going to the bars they used to get kicked out of in high school.

[8] Johnny Waterbottle's name isn't really Johnny Waterbottle or Jody Waterfall or Joanie Wonderwall or any of the names that he will be referred to in the following pages, but we had a teacher in grade school call him a many number of these names and not only did the nicknames stick, but they evolved over time, becoming so stupid that they will likely follow him for his entire life. (In fact, names like this are going to come up a lot through the rest of this tall tale, so unless it's relevant information, I'm going to pass over any ridiculous name, without any sort of explanation, and I hope you do the same.)

who's that other girl who's always hanging out at Mic's house?"

[Background. I am the oldest of four siblings. Following me, there is a brother (the vegan bodybuilder I mentioned earlier), a sister who looks just like a tall version of my mother (a pale, red-headed person), and my youngest sister (a 4'10" darker complexioned person with very thick, very straight black hair who was born in Central America and was adopted by my parents before she was two years old). Long story short, she doesn't look like anyone else in our household. Observing this and finding out why she doesn't look anything like the rest of us is something most people can get out of the way upon first meeting our family. Honestly, most people couldn't care less. This is America, the greatest melting pot in the history of the world. And sure, the original European settlers pretty much wiped out anybody that even remotely resembles my sister, but the majority of people around here just assume she's from "somewhere down by Mexico" and call it a day.]

But not our friend Dave. Dave has known me and my family since middle school. We'd been doing stupid shit together, along with the rest of these fools, for almost 10 years at this point. He has seen all of my siblings hundreds of times. And while, yes—my sisters are younger than us—he's had dinner at our house. He's been on long car rides with us. But somehow, the concept that my youngest sister is, in fact, my youngest sister has never occurred to him. Come to think of it, I guess his frame of reference on what a family looks like is pretty straight and narrow. Growing up, the majority of our friends had pretty monochromatic families. But by the time you're in your mid-20s, you should have enough life experience to know that other people's life experiences are different from your own. Or am I naive in thinking that people walk through life observing things around them with curiosity and empathy? Aren't your early 20s supposed to be about talking to other people in their early 20s who grew up in a different environment than your own, about exploring "new" ideas, assuming those ideas are important, validating the importance of those ideas with the other 20-year-olds around you, and ponying up to make a change in this world, *man?* Isn't that the point of college, *man?*

I don't think Dave ever graduated college—neither did I—but he went! And how could he have not met someone, in his three freshman years, whose upbringing was just different enough to broaden his horizons? But this situation, in particular, is not about Dave's narrowness of experience, it's about the fact that he never even considered the possibility that siblings could be related but not by blood.

So…where were we?

"Hey, J, who's that girl who's always hanging out at Mic's house?" Dave asks.

"That's Mic's sister," replies Jody Waterbottle.

"No, I know who Mic's sister is. But who's that other girl who's always hanging out at Mic's house?" re-asks Dave.

"She is also Mic's sister," replies Jody.

"No, I know Mic's sister. Who's that other girl?"

At this point, Johnny Teacup realizes that Dave cannot, on his own, comprehend what he's being told, leaving Johnny with two options:

He could explain the entirety of the situation to Dave, making him feel dumb for not realizing that I had an adopted sister that he knows personally and has known for the past 12 years.

or

He could lie to Dave, giving him the gift of drama and the satisfaction of having a little secret—something Dave loves to have, but can never keep.

Johnny chooses the latter, and rightfully so. But he can't come up with the perfect thing to tell Dave on such short notice, so he stalls, adding to the drama.

"Who's the other girl?" Dave asks. "The dark-haired girl."

"*Shh!* Don't you know…we don't talk about it, man," Johnny says.

"What do you mean?" asks Dave, worried he's missed something, which he most certainly has.

"That's Mic's sister. But we don't talk about it."

"*What?!*" Dave can't handle himself, so excited to be let in on something that "we don't talk about."

"I'll tell you later," Johnny replies, buying himself more time.

They pick me up as we head to meet the rest of the gang at Shoes. Dave is riding shotgun in Johnny's Cutlass Supreme (the same car Johnny's mother drove to drop us off for soccer practice) and Dave is acting very quiet and polite. This is very suspicious behavior for someone who usually greets friends he hasn't seen in a while with jolly profanities and a big dumb grin on his face.

I look at Johnny through the rearview mirror as we both acknowledge the fact that Dave is acting strange. But Johnny nods to assure me that Dave's behavior is due to an active gag that I will be informed of at a later time and place. The smile that is frantically leaking out of Mr. Wattlebottle's attempted poker face lets me know that he is the proud parent of this gag—he is glowing.

"So, how's your family?" asks Dave.

"They seem good. Good to see everybody," I say. "How's yours?"

"They're fine," he responds. He takes a long pause, looking out the window. "How's your brother?" (Again, this is very unusual behavior for someone who exclusively talks about themselves.)

"He's fine. He wrapped up school, but I bet he'll just try to find a way to live in a tent and garden full time," I reply. Looking to Johnny for some clue as to where this is going.

"Cool, cool," Dave responds nonchalantly. (He's just being cordial. You know, the opposite of the way he usually is. No big deal. Nothing to see here.)

"How's your sister?" he asks, in an awkward, overly-casual way—like a crazy person who's trying to play it cool, the way he's seen "playing it cool" in movies.

"How's my sister?" (Now I'm very suspicious. My sisters are 12 and 14 at this point. Does he even know their names? Why does he care?) "Which sister?" I ask.

Dave looks at Johnny then back at the road again—Johnny never taking his eyes off the road.

"I don't know," Dave says. "Both of 'em!" pausing then asking again, "How're your *sisters*?" (Really emphasizing *"sisters"* like he's trying to signal something to me.)

"Jesus Christ," Johnny mumbles under his breath.

It's funny, looking back at it because Dave's such a dumbass. But at the time, I was mad. I'm not 100% sure why. But I was mad. Confused more than anything, but furious nonetheless.

There's a quirk that exists in the brains of all sorts of people around here (myself included)—and I'm sure it's been written about by people who *actually* study the behavior of people—but where I come from, if you feel like someone is leaning towards disrespecting your family, you may consider it necessary to physically harm them, just to make sure it doesn't happen again.

Now, this isn't a rational reaction. A rational reaction would be to say, "Fuck that dude," and avoid contact with this disrespect because honestly, it's just words. Disrespect isn't great, but there's no reason to make the situation worse by getting physical. And beyond that, *maybe* you exchange some words with the offender—maybe even heated words—words that could maybe, *eventually* turn into a physical altercation. But the words should come first, right?

Right. But, no. This motherfucker just asked 'how my sisters were doing' and now I'm thinking that I'm going to hit him in the face when we get out of the car.

That's irrational. That's flawed behavior.

And that's my gut instinct. I don't act on this instinct. I have self-control, but I hear about incidents like this all the time throughout, Ohio, Michigan, Kentucky, West Virginia, Pennsylvania, and Western New York State.

"This dude looked at my brother weird, so we torched his car."

"This dude was talking to my mother, so we paralyzed him."

"I heard from a guy that this dude said something to another guy about how my brother said something that he didn't say, so we put his body in the trunk of a stolen car and drove it into a lake."

This is crazy behavior. It's not as organized as a mafia movie. It's not as civil as gang violence. It's crazy behavior. It's about pride and respect, but it's always reactionary. It's never for any long-term goal. It's country, but there's no strategy to it. It's just knucklehead stuff that escalates far too quickly.

Where country-ass rage may be a little slower to bubble over in the Deep South or Out West, Northwest Ohio is the perfect storm of mentalities and climate that make even the smallest social interactions with the wrong people a very dangerous game.

But what is it that makes people this way?

Is it the sludge-stained snow of the long winters and the alcohol/drugs that come with passing that time? Is it the broken promise of a steady job at the plant when you graduate combined with the summer you spent shoveling shit out of Uncle Danny's pig pit? Is it the fact that even if you DID make more money, the "government would just take it all" and you'd never be able to get the water-front room on Put-in-Bay this summer, let alone during the Kid Rock concert? Is it paying an outrageous amount of money to go to Ohio State while knowing that if you were born 80 miles north, you could've gotten an in-state scholarship to the University of Michigan?

"No. Why would I want to go to Michigan? Ohio State's the best!"

"Sorry—I'm just making the argument. All I'm saying is that if you were from Michigan, you'd probably be a Michigan fan and not an Ohio State fan. That's all I'm saying."

"No, I wouldn't. Because Ohio State's the *best!* Michigan fucking blows, bro. What, you like Michigan or something? What, are you a faggot? Huh? You like suckin' dick, bro? Michigan faggot!"

"Relax, dude. Jesus."

This is an interaction that I had a few years back with a person I haven't seen since high school. He is an adult man with a house, a job, four children, and a lovely, though chaotic, wife (who also went to our high school). He is a seemingly sensible person outside of talking about Ohio State football. Other than the walls of his basement, this OSU fandom seems to play no effect on any other part of his life. His family decorates in the *"These Are My Things"* motif with just a splash of *"I Love the Beach"* in the bathrooms. Normal stuff.

But when you're at a bar in your hometown around the holidays, and everyone you've ever met is there and having a good time, things may start to get a little loose. You might find yourself drinking a little too much and having your 16-year-old son pick you up. You might tell your 8th-grade girlfriend that you love her.[9] Or hell, maybe you'll call some dude you haven't seen in 10 years a "Michigan faggot." You could be more creative, you could use a better turn-of-phrase, but why would you? Creativity and the ability to form sentences are pretentious, and you aint some "Michigan faggot."

You're from Ohio. Fuck Michigan! This state bleeds Ohio State scarlet—so you do too! We're *red*, they're *blue*. We're right, they're left. We're the best, they suck. "Those whiny liberals don't even know how to drive!"

While we're at it, I want to make a quick note about this legendary college sports rivalry.

The town in which I grew up, is almost exactly equidistant to Ann Arbor, Michigan ("24.6 square miles, surrounded by reality," home to Michigan University) and Columbus, Ohio home of *THE* Ohio State University. (I emphasize the *"THE"* because that's the way Ohio State fans pronounce it. My father attended Bowling Green State University. He loves to correct people by saying he attended *THE* Bowling Green State University. Easily one of my favorite bits.)

---

[9] She's an adult now. She *WAS* your girlfriend when the *BOTH* of you were in 8th grade. But she's an adult now. Relax.

Michigan and Ohio State's rivalry is very well documented and I'm sure you can read hundreds of books on the subject. But I believe the colors associated with these teams and the weight that certain folks give this rivalry contribute to the strange family-style animosity that shapes the minds of people that grow up in this part of the world.

I for one, totally enjoy a good sports rivalry, especially in college sports. I love the bands. I love a super fan. I love some good shit talk. I love the tradition of it all. But things take a turn when people who didn't even go to the school decide that they are going to turn some well-natured shit-talk at a bar into 2nd-degree murder.

A Michigan fan walking into an Ohio State bar knows that he's going to be given a hard time, and honestly, he's asking for it. Otherwise, he wouldn't have gone there in the first place. Listen, Michigan rarely beats Ohio State in a game of football[10], so to me, the only appropriate action for an Ohio State fan to take when running into said Michigan fan in a bathroom is to apologize for the ass-whooping last Thanksgiving. Both fans can acknowledge the struggle that Michigan has had, have a chuckle, and move on.[11]

But, because of the pageantry, because of the group mentality, because of the opportunity to go over the top with sports fandom, for every 100 normal, socially acceptable, low-key interactions an Ohio State fan could have with a

---

[10] Until recently. Thanksgiving weekend 2021 was a spanking. Good for Jim Harbaugh.

[11] And like I said, Michigan *did* win in 2021. If they continue to win against Ohio State, I would love to get some quantitative analysis regarding the psyche of Ohio based sports fans and the way the relate to the rest of the world. Let me see some pre-2021 numbers. Let me see some post 2021 numbers. Let me see some charts. Let me see some graphs.

Michigan fan, there is *one* weirdo who's already ready to boil over before any sort of interaction even takes place.

This one weirdo gets so jazzed by the amount of high fives that he gets after a touchdown that within the first quarter of the game he is ready to literally ride or die for anyone else in this bar who's also wearing a red shirt. He's never felt this level of acceptance outside of this bar, so this is where he'll stay.

It can be a thing of beauty, feeling connected this way. But if you have no sense of self, other than this devotion to your team and fellow fans, then those fellow fans become your family. And you would do anything for your family. And you want them to know how devoted you are. That's why they like you, right? Because of your devotion to the team. You want them to see that you would do anything for them. You want them to like you. You would do anything for the team, anything for your family. You'd kill a man. Then they'd know that you were serious about the team. *That's* how serious you are. They can trust you. They'll invite you to the bar to watch the game next time. Because you're the *biggest* fan. A fan that would kill a man for his team. They'll love you for it. They'll cheer for *YOU*. Because *YOU* taught that Michigan fan a lesson. Don't mess with the Buckeyes.

O-H!

I-O!

It's almost religious, really.

You do things not because it makes sense to do them, but because you doing those things makes you a part of the group. You're plural. You're *US*. You're *WE*. You're a part of the team. And *OUR* team is *US* against everyone else.

If you're not pulling for Ohio State, then you must be pulling for Michigan.

If you're not with us, then you're against us. And if you're against us, then we're against you.

Because *YOUR* team is who *YOU* are. And *MY* team is who *I* am. It's personal.

We're RED. You're BLUE. We're right. You're left. We're the best. You suck. "You whiny liberals don't even know how to drive!"

Now, I *do* think those colors, RED and BLUE, play more of a part in Ohio's culture than we give them credit for. Those colors are so engrained in the psyche of people around here, that I wouldn't be surprised to see a similar color divide on a voting map in a Presidential Election.

I know some of you fools in Columbus are like, "Hey Mic! Fuck you. Just because I'm an Ohio State fan doesn't mean I voted for Trump!"

To which I'd respond, "Hey! Fuck you! I'm not talking about *you* assholes. You guys are the educated few. You guys went to school there or your kids went to school there or something. You value public education and healthcare and social justice. Bullshit like that. I'm talking about everyone else."

I'm simply saying, odds are, in Ohio, if you voted for Trump, you probably also have an Ohio State flag out in front of the house. Why? Because you're a *winner*. And you want everyone else to know that you're a winner. So you put stickers and flags and signs in your yard that let people know, "Hey! This house is full of winners! And if you don't like it, then you're not with us. And if you're not with us, you're against us. And if you're against us, then we're against *you*. We're RED. You're BLUE. We're RIGHT. You're LEFT. We're the BEST. You SUCK. And you only hate us 'cus we're WINNERS. You whiny liberals don't even know how to drive."

Now, I will also say, there are plenty of people in Michigan who voted for Trump. Plenty of those people used to vote for the blue-collar democrat as well. But when the blue-collar candidate doesn't exist, and the unions don't have the pull that they used to, and the factory closed, and you still don't have potable water in the house, then you vote for the candidate with whom you have most in common: the Wrestlemania candidate. (No disrespect to the unions or Wrestlemania.) And if everyone around you is voting for the Wrestlemania candidate, then you're a part of that team. And it feels good to be a part of a team. And hell, if that team wins, that makes you a winner, and man, it feels good to win. It's been a long time since parts of Michigan had a win.

Sure, there are other parts of Michigan that stay winning. Those people have beautifully restored wooden boats and shit. I'm not talking about that. I'm talking about the Lake Erie side of Michigan. The side that could use a win.

And man, once they get that win, it's hard to convince them to vote the other way. Even if that candidate is so slimy that he goes back on every promise he made to you, it'd be hard not to vote for him. Because up here, politicians going back on their promises is beyond typical. It's classic. It's expected. And at least this guy's a winner! That makes you a winner.

Those whiny liberals hate to see him win. They hate to see *us* win. That's why he's our guy. Because if you're not with us, then you must be against us. We're *red*. You're *blue*.

And honestly, props to Trump's people for seeing the basic instincts of a vulnerable population and just running with that. No policy, nothin'. Just cheer-able slogans that are less than four syllables and team colors. And boy, when those colors are also associated with the home team, and the opposing party's colors match those of your rival across the border, you're looking at a huge ride-or-die voting demographic. And even if they're not as *huge* as the voter turnout for the last champ, they're still loud as hell and happy to put a sign in the yard, or at the very least, call someone a "faggot" at a bar for wearing a blue hat.

Sorry for the tangent. Back to it.

—

So, Dave asks me how my sisters are doing, I control my Ohio-born rage and decide not to take a swing at him when we get out of the car. The bar is crowded with college students that are home for the holidays and the townies that were going to be there regardless.

Later in the evening, Johnny makes a point of pulling me aside at the bar. He noticed that I was still hot over Dave's question about my sisters. He explains to me that, despite Dave knowing my family for years, he hadn't put together the fact that my youngest sister is adopted and looks nothing like the rest of us. It's possible that he didn't even know that she was my sister at all. I laugh and ask a few questions, both of us acknowledging how strange Dave's mind can be. I keep waiting for the punchline of the bit and realize that Jody Waterslide is asking me for permission to tell Dave some crazy shit that he will then believe for the foreseeable future. I see the sparkle in Johnny's eyes as I realize the bit has already begun.

The evening moves on. A once rowdy crowd of college students has thinned to the regulars at the bar and the homies at a grouping of tables in the back corner. We cash out, say our goodbyes to Tracy at the bar, and head for home.

On the ride home, Dave is acting strange again. We've all had a long evening, but he seems distracted by something. And he sits in the backseat of Johnny's car with an uncharacteristically somber demeanor.

He doesn't say much, he just looks out the window at the streetlights. Again, this is very unusual behavior for someone whose normal routine after a night of indulgence with some friends is to recount every conversation and action that happened just hours before.

"You guys remember when Fish said that he was happy to see everybody? You remember that? Yeah, what a little bitch!"

"Hey…hey! You guys remember when Tyler and Travis came over and they were telling us about working down in Columbus and stuff and then we did shots? Remember that?"

Stuff like that.

But not tonight. Tonight, he appears to be pondering the existence of life itself. Tonight, he thinks how strange it is to be anything at all.

I'm concerned at this point and break the silence by asking,

"Hey…you doin' all right back there?"

To which he responds,

"Me…I'm great. I'm just thankful, you know. Thinkin' about my family. And where I come from. I'm just thankful, you know. But how're you doing? Everything all right? Family OK? Your dad OK?"

"Yeah man, we're fine," I respond. I look at Johnny who is shaking with excitement. He obviously told Dave something wild and is thrilled with himself. "But thanks for asking," I add.

At this point, Johnny Waterbottle had just taken a sip of water from his namesake. But his body was still spasming with joy and he couldn't do anything but spit the water all over the steering wheel.

"Shit, Jody! Are you all right?" Dave asks from the back seat, suddenly overtaken with compassion and concern for everyone's wellbeing.

We get to Dave's house—his parents' house, rather. Though Dave is just home for the holidays, he will move back into this house when he's done with school this year. Five years is plenty of time to try and graduate with some sort of undergraduate degree, and despite being "not quite finished," he's not even close to being finished with his sophomore year. So, reluctantly, he will shut it down, move back in with his folks for a bit, regroup, and move somewhere out west with nothing but his guitar, a skateboard, and the clothes he can fit in a backpack—like the beginning of a 90s coming-of-age style movie. Lot of horns and surf guitars on the soundtrack.

And honestly, that's probably what he should've done in the first place. But around here, if you don't go to college, then what are you doing? You're working at a restaurant downtown or working at the plant. For the rest of your life.[12]

If you don't want to work at the restaurant or the plant, you go to college. Like your parents. Like you're supposed to, right? But when you get out of college, those high-payin-big-timin-college-graduate jobs aren't what they used to be and you realize that you're just starting your adult life 4-6 years later, 15-20lbs heavier, and in debt up to your eyeballs with an institution that allowed you to learn some new information and get drunk with your friends for half a decade.

If you can hustle, you can get you a job that may turn into a big-girl job. *Or* you can move back home and take time to regroup. *Or* you can put off student loans by continuing to go to school in hopes that one day, someone gets elected and forgives the cost of your magnificent education.

---

[12] Or until it closes, or the robots take your job. The news will try to tell you that the immigrants took your job, but we all know it's the robots. By the way, where are all the anti-robot protestors at? Everybody was showing up with guns protesting stay-at-home orders during a pandemic. Meanwhile, while you're out of work, the big boss man is hiring robots to do your shit for you. Where my anti-robot signs at?

But in this moment, Dave's not thinking about the future. It's not really his thing. But he steps out of the car. Leans down to my window, and says, "Hey Johnny, thanks for the ride. And hey, Mic, hang in there. And tell your dad I said 'Hey.' He's a good man."

We roll out of the driveway and I turn to Johnny Waterworld. He's in tears with a grin from ear to ear. He's laughing so hard that he has to pull over. I'm sure some neighbor considered calling the cops as we sat idling in the cutlass in front of some brick, pond-front, McMansion in Dave's parent's neighborhood.

"What the fuck was that?" I ask Johnny.

"I'm just shocked," he says. "I want him to be smarter than he is, Mic."

"What did you tell him?" I ask.

Johnny attempts to compose himself. "So…Dave doesn't understand that your sister is adopted, right?" he explains. "Like…he may not know that 'adoption' exists. But he knows that she's your sister. Because I told him, right?"

"Okaaay…" I nod, waiting to see where this goes.

"Once I saw that he wasn't getting it, I started to think: what could be a good explanation as to why your very small, dark-haired, dark-complexioned, Native American sister doesn't look anything like your ginger-ass family?" he explains.

"Go on…"

"So, I told him that years ago, when we were kids, your mother had an affair with a little Caribbean man from Toledo. Like, a *really* little Caribbean man. And she got pregnant and didn't tell your dad about this little guy, so when she gave birth to this tiny little brown baby, your father was flabbergasted. But he's never said a thing about it. He never addressed that she's obviously not his child-by-blood, but he raised her as if she was his own and never said a word about it. Your mother was so impressed that she broke off the affair with the man in Toledo and has been devoted to your father ever since."

"What?" I ask. "And he believed that?"

"Of course, he did. It's sensational. He wants to believe it because it's so good!"

"But that's outrageous!" I reply. "My sister looks nothing like the combination of a red-headed lady and a little Caribbean man. And you're telling me he actually believes this? Like he didn't go, 'Ah…I bet Johnny's just fuckin' with me. She's probably just adopted or something.' You think he *actually* believes it?"

"No doubt. I had to hold off on giving the little man a name to make the story seem more realistic."

"More realistic?!" I exclaim. "This was the more realistic version? How does he think that you know so much about my mother's sex life?"

"No idea," Johnny says. "But he was thrilled as I was telling him. I told him, 'Hey…we don't talk about it, so keep your mouth shut. I don't even think Mic knows.'"

“If I didn’t know, then how in the world would you know!?”

“No idea,” he responds, wiping the tears from his eyes. “I want to say Dave’s a smart guy. But man, he’s just not.”

He starts the car. And we start to drive back to my parents’ house. Both of us exchange glances back and forth as to how Dave could believe such an outrageous story without even questioning it.

“You know Dave can’t keep a secret, right? Is he going to tell everyone that my mother had an affair with this little guy?” I ask.

“I don’t think so. I made a real point of being very serious. And he practically begged me to tell him, so I think that he thinks he’s got a really juicy secret and if he lets that cat out of the bag, the secret’s not as juicy anymore.”

“So, you think he will prioritize the juiciness of the secret?” I ask.

“Definitely. But I’d give your mom a heads-up just in case.”

“Jesus. She’s going to love this,” I say, rolling my eyes. My mother *loves* being in on a bit almost as much as Dave.

We pull up to my house and we side hug/handshake across the center console, as homies do. I step out and close the car door.

Johnny leans over the console to look out the window at me and says,

"Hey, Mic, hang in there. And tell your dad I say 'Hey.' He's a good man."

We both laugh and I start to walk inside as he backs out of the driveway.

I turn back around and jog back to his car on the street.

"Hey Jody, you said you had to hold back on giving that little man a name to make the story realistic."

"Yeah."

"What were you going to call him?" I ask.

"What?"

"What were you going to name this man?"

"Cornelius," he says. "The little man's name is Cornelius."

I look down and shake my head. He turns on the radio. The Ambrosia song, "Biggest Part of Me," is on.

"God...I love this song!" He says as he turns the radio up to 10, shifts into gear, and drives off into the sunrise.

—

So, that's what my mother was talking about when she asked if Dave "still thought my sister was a little bastard child."

"You think he's playing you guys?" my mother asks.

“What do you mean?” I ask back.

“Dave. Do you think he’s actually really smart and he’s just going along with all the crazy stuff you tell him?” she asks.

“No way,” I say.

“I don’t know,” my brother interjects. “He’s like the combination of the Dustin Hoffman and Tom Cruise characters in *Rain Man*. Like…his brain is strange. And he’s good at some things. I guess. But he’s also a hothead. But he’s a nice guy. Right? Or maybe he’s not. Maybe he’s actually a nice guy but he wants people to think that he’s not a nice guy? I don’t know. Now that I say it out loud, he’s not really like Rain Man at all. I bet he’s really bad at math.”

“Oh, he’s probably horrible at math,” my dad interjects—the only thing he has to add to another conversation about the strangeness of Dave.

“So, Dave gets in this morning, and then what, y’all are gonna go to Shoes?” my mother asks.

“Can I come?” my dad asks. “Just kidding. But seriously.”

“Oh…we used to go there all the time before you nerds showed up,” my mom adds.

“Hell, I’m sure we used to take ‘em,” my dad says to her. “At least the two of you,” he gestures to me and my brother.

“Definitely,” I say.

"No way!" my mother argues. "We wouldn't have taken the boys to the bar when they were little."

"I'm pretty sure we had a baby shower there," my dad says. "Maybe two. I bet we had both showers there."

"No way," my mother responds. She remembers the baby showers. She remembers the good times. She remembers *everything.*

"So, you're going to Shoes, here in a sec, then the funeral's tomorrow?

"Funeral's this afternoon. You're more than welcome to come."

"Outrageous," my father says. "St. Pat's?"

"Nope. Put-in-Bay," my brother says.

"Jesus. You're putting the casket on the ferry?" my dad asks.

"It's what he would've wanted," I respond.

"Long live Arthur McFischerson," my father says.

"You guys are sick," my mother responds. "I can't believe Connie's okay with all of this. And his siblings? You're sure everyone knows?"

"It was in the *paper*," my brother says, laughing.

"Yeah, that's awesome," my father says.

[*The Citizen*—formerly *The Republican Citizen*—is the daily source of news back home. While newspapers all over the country have closed their doors, *The Citizen* thrives as the single source of "hey, if they printed it, it must be true" in our midsize Midwestern city. What the paper lacks in hard-hitting investigative journalism, it makes up for tenfold in "Page Six" style, one-off op-eds, and a colorfully written public record section.

The Citizen's Public Record, or "The Docket" as it is lovingly referred to by locals, is ripe with thesaurus heavy wordage.

If something's been stolen, it's been "pilfered."

It's not a fight, it's a "fracas."

"Local teens questioned for area shenanigans."

You love to see it![13]]

"I can't believe all this," my mother says. "This is a lot of effort."

"Well, Mom," chimes my brother, "wouldn't you want *your* friends to put forth some effort at *your* funeral?"

"Yeah, have a little decency, *Mom*," I say.

"Yeah, babe! Have a little respect," my father adds, stretching his arms out like a Catholic priest. "May the

[13] "You love to see it!" Was/Is one of Fish's favorite catch-all phrases.

souls of the faithfully departed, through the mercy of Arthur Fischer and his stupid friends, rest in peace. Amen."[14]

"Long live the Fish," I say. "But seriously, you all are more than welcome to come to Shoes for the thing. I'm sure Tracy would get a kick out of seeing y'all out at the bar again, and I know Connie would really appreciate the support. This has been a *very* hard time."

"I can only imagine," my dad responds as my mother shakes her head. "She only mentioned it briefly when I went to get my hair cut the other day. Must be hard to talk about."

"All of you are sick," my mother repeats.

"We'll be there," says my dad while looking at my mother. "It's the least we could do."

"Same," says my brother. "Never been so excited for a funeral."

---

[14] Such a Catholic joke.

Hometown Heroes

For the next couple hours, I sit around and catch up with my family—usually something that occurs over the course of an entire holiday-sized weekend, but due to the circumstances, we spend the next couple hours talking about my sisters' boyfriends, my grandparents, the political landscape, sports projections, and the weather. Quite a lot to pack into a couple of hours, *especially* if you're long talkers, like us. But it's April: football's not even close to happening and you can only talk about pre-post-season sports for so long. Northwest Ohio is mostly Detroit sports fans, Cleveland Sports fans, or Cincinnati sports fans, but every once in a while, you see a die-hard Pittsburgh Steelers fan. They couldn't care less about any other Pittsburgh team, but you'd better believe that their giant-ass satellite dish in their postage-stamp-sized, chain-link-fenced yard is painted like the Steelers logo. Why? Because they don't want to be mistaken for some Cleveland Browns lovin' *loser*. They're *winners*! And you're gonna know it!

"Steelers gon' win! Steelers gon' win!"[15]

---

[15] Side story: I was in a hit-and-run car accident as a teenager. (This is NOT a dramatic story. Everyone's fine. RELAX.) *But,* as this Chevy sedan tries to pass me in opposing traffic, it sideswipes my entire car, takes off my driver's side mirror, then spins itself around 180 degrees so the other driver and I are looking right at each other—driver's side headlight to driver's side headlight. The driver slowly turns his steering wheel and pulls up to the side of my car to see if I'm all right. As the driver and I make eye contact, both of us realizing that he wasn't about to stop and exchange

As far as professional sports go, my family is a blend of the Detroit and Cleveland fan bases. Pulling for the Browns when they're trying, the Lions when it's Christmas, the Cavs when they're winning, and the Pistons when they're not. I pull for the Tigers. My grandpa pulls for the Indians. And everybody pulls for the Toledo Mudhens.

"While we're talkin' sports, let's send it out to our sportsman in the field, Daniel "Double Dip" DuBois!"

> *"HEY, GANG! WHAT A BEAUTIFUL DAY FOR BASEBALL! THOSE MUDHENS ARE LOOKIN' GREAT SO FAR AND AFTER THAT LONG AND VICTORIOUS POSTSEASON, IT LOOKS LIKE THE HENS' LEADERSHIP IS LOOKIN' FOR ANOTHER RUN AT THE AAA CHAMPIONSHIP. WILL THEY COME UP SHORT OR WILL THEY DOUBLE DIP INTO THAT SWEET, SWEET WINNER SAUCE? DON'T GO ANYWHERE. THIS IS WCWA 1230 AM, HOME OF …*
>
> *YOUR*
>
> *TOLEDO MUDHENS."*

Daniel DuBois a.k.a. Doobs a.k.a. Double Dip DuBois (his work-in-progress radio personality name) is one of the remaining homies who still lives back home. And while he doesn't currently work at the local sports radio station, it is his destiny. His voice hits somewhere between a cartoon auctioneer, a Jimmy Stewart character, and a post-

---

insurance info, the dude in the back seat of the car rolls down his window and yells "*Steelers gon' win! Steelers gon' win!*" Then they drive off into the night.

pubescent Mickey Mouse, so listening to his podcast, where he talks through whatever game he's watching at the time, is a real treat. His hope is that this unpaid commitment to sportscasting will catch the attention of some radio executive somewhere down the line, but until then he will continue to talk shit about LeBron James and the injustices happening all across the sports spectrum.[16]

Doobs is also a very meticulous person. He likes things the way he likes them.

Peanut Butter and Jelly: "Crunchy peanut butter? Do you have creamy peanut butter instead? No? No, thanks. I'll have nothing at all."

Cheeseburger: "You only have Pepper Jack? No American? No thanks. I'll have nothing...No, I don't want anything."

Pop[17] : "You're telling me you *only* have Pepsi? No Coke? No. No. I'm fine...No...Why would I want a Pepsi? Who wants a Pepsi? No, it's ok. I'll just kill myself."

There is a culinary rarity that exists in this part of the country, exclusively. They call it a *Shredded Chicken*

---

[16] He's never forgiven LeBron for "taking his talents to South Beach." In fact, he decided he was no longer a Cavs fan after LeBron came back to Cleveland. He felt personally betrayed and vowed to never root for LeBron or the Cavs ever again. This kind of commitment to a team (and commitment to the beef you have with a team) is what makes Ohio the way that it is. It's ride or die. If you betray the team, you're out. Even if you come back and win that team—that city—their first championship in 50 years, you're still out. Once a traitor, always a traitor. (And in the eyes of Doobs, betrayal is unforgivable.)

[17] Soda. You know what I'm talking about. Don't act like you don't.

Sandwich. It exists in an alternate dimension to a *Sloppy Joe* between Lima and Toledo, Ohio. They're distributed at Dairy Dips, 8th Grade Catholic Confirmation Receptions, and High School Graduation Parties. It consists of pulled chicken (ideally from a can), cream of mushroom soup, and salt on a potato roll/white bread hamburger bun. To make such a sandwich, you put the chicken, soup, and salt in a Crock-Pot and let it sit for an unimportant amount of time. Then you put that warm shredded-chicken/mushroom-soup mixture onto the white bread bun, and that's it. No condiments, nothing. Beside this sandwich, you will find Ballreich's Chips—a comically oily and *very* salty potato chip in a plain white bag. If you really want to take this meal to a place where you evolve into a native Northwest Ohioan, you would order some sort of "pop" to balance the pH of this alkalinity-fest. It doesn't really matter what flavor or brand, but the apostles of the Insane Clown Posse would urge you to try Faygo.

Doobs is the personification of a *Shredded Chicken Sandwich*. Not to say he doesn't have taste; he just likes what he likes, and nothing else. It may not make sense to anyone else, but he knows his truth to be true, and that is enough for him. Doobs may be, more than Shredded Chicken itself, the most Northwest Ohio-y product to ever exist.

This commitment to your own truths and ideals, regardless of whether or not they're actually true *or* ideal, comes with its struggles, but it also comes with a commitment to the friends and family that enable this behavior.

And it's that commitment to friendship and towniness that makes Doobs and our friend Murphy (the most steady and functional townie there ever was) the perfect combo to organize a wake at a bar.

Like most of us, Murphy and Doobs don't see each other as often as they used to, despite the fact that they still live about a mile apart from each other. While everyone else is excited to see the gang around the holidays, Murphy and Doobs see this as just another evening at the bar. They're there when everyone meets up, but the two of them don't chum it up with each other. It's almost like they've seen each other one too many times. There's never been a falling out, but I could see how Doobs' illogical hard-nosedness and Murph's logical levelheadedness would run into each other after the dust settles—both parties acknowledging that they don't need to spend every waking minute together, and it's ok if we just "see ya 'round."

But nothing brings old friends together quite like a funeral.

Murphy, in this particular situation (the organization of a wake at a bar), is a natural funeral director. It comes so naturally to him, that he considers going into the mortuary arts after all of this, then reconsiders, remembering that dealing with your stupid buddies is different than dealing with real death within families that aren't your own. He could handle it. He's a champ and a very empathetic person, but it's a whole thing, and nobody's got time for a whole thing. And if you're going to go to the trouble of going through a whole thing, do you want that whole thing to lead up to the direction of traditional funeral proceedings? Probably not. So maybe one day, he'll go and do a whole thing. But he would say that he feels good where he's at. And that he likes doing what he's doing. I envy that very much.

Doobs, in this particular situation (the organization of a wake at a bar), is the detail man. If you want your boozy wake and your lakefront funeral to look and feel like the real thing, he's your man. Table decorations, cold-cut snack plates, the words "IM SORRY FOR YOUR LOSS" hanging from the rafters in gold-glitter, party-store, cardboard birthday font.

He's the guy you see when you first walk in. He's wearing the extra-large 2001-NBA-draft-pick-style black pinstripe suit (jarring for a person who doesn't own jeans. He prefers the elasticity and airflow that comes with a pair of athletic shorts). He says, "Thank you for coming," to everyone, even if he knows them personally, and could strike up a fluid conversation with a complete stranger without fumbling the ball. But this is not a time for conversation, this is a time for mourning. And he's happy to politely remind you to keep your voice down.

These two dudes are the hometown heroes of the weekend and beyond. Putting together a pirate-style wake at a bar is no easy task, but it would be an impossible task if it weren't for Tracy at Shoes and her daughter, Meghan.

Meghan and I worked together at a bar on Put-in-Bay some years ago. She graduated from high school a few years before me. We grew up down the street from each other but never really met until we both found ourselves working at this real gem on the island. While working in the service industry, I always found myself washing dishes, moving ice around, or maybe working a fryer in the back. But Meghan is the daughter of Ms. Tracy, possibly the best bartender in the history of the game. Meghan's grandpa started Shoes. She's a legacy and a hell of a bartender herself. She's tried her hand at other things. She's moved away a few times, toured with a few bands, etc. But as Tracy started to slow down, Meghan eventually returned to fulfill her duties. Not because she had to, but because she wanted to. It's Shakespearian. It's Biblical. It's beautiful.

Once the idea of using Shoes as a location for the wake comes up, the rest of the gang is set on it. I don't like to call in favors, but this seemed like something Meghan and Tracy could be into. So about two months ago, I flip through the contacts in my old flip phone and find Meghan's number.

I thought that if I remembered correctly, Meghan was pretty old-school like her mom and wouldn't hate a phone call from an old friend. But it's kind of nerve-racking to call up someone you haven't talked to in ten years. My brother said she was still working at the bar, so I knew she was around, but you never know with people.

The phone rings and rings a little longer. I debate hanging up and gathering my thoughts, but then I hear that familiar voice.

"Mr. Fox. How the hell are ya?"

Perfect. I take a huge sigh of relief. She sounds just like her mother.

"Meghan! Been too long, bud. How is everything?"

"It's good my friend. I'm good. You back in town yet?"

I laugh. "Not yet. But that's part of why I'm calling."

“Oh, you’ll be back. You gotta go away so you can come back, sir.” She speaks like Marcie talking to Peppermint Patty. “So, what’s up?”

I explain to her the situation in a Charlie Brown-like fashion—excited about the possibilities of something great but expecting to be let down.

“Holy shit, that sounds hilarious. I remember that guy! Connie’s kid, right?” she responds.

“Yep! That’s him,” I say.

“I don’t think we’ve held a wake here before. At least not an official one. Are all the old buddies coming?”

“That’s the idea. But no pressure, you know. I don’t want to put you guys out,” I say.

“Let me talk to mom about it,” she says. “She was just over at Connie’s getting her hair done this morning. I’m sure we can rent out the back room for you guys, at the very least. How many people are we talking about?”

“Maybe 30? Including his family,” I say.

“Holy shit, his family’s coming?!” she asks. “Connie’s in on it?! So, this is a situation.”

“I mean, you think Connie would miss her own son’s funeral?” I reply.

She laughs. “OK, so is there going to be a full-blown funeral service?”

“At our old stomping grounds,” I say.

“Wait…like…”

“Yep.”

“You’re going to put the casket on a boat?” she asks.

“Either that or we’re going to try and get it on the ferry,” I respond, laughing.

“Jesus Christ,” she says. “OK, if Connie’s in, then we’re in. I’ll talk to mom. Keep us posted.”

“Amazing,” I say. “You guys are the best.”

“This is insane. Mom’s gonna flip. I’ll call you later. And hey…sorry about Fish. He was a good man.”

I laugh and she hangs up the phone.

Perfect.

—

I love securing a good setting. After we lock in Shoes for the wake, I start to brainstorm ways to get a casket onto an island in the middle of the lake.

Our first thought is to rent a boat, but Lake Erie is no small pontoon-boat lake. It’s a big-ass lake. As a child, I thought it was the ocean. It might as well be—if you sail across it, you’re in a different country.

Once we realize that none of us know how to sail or drive a big boy boat that's capable of getting across some open waters, we set our eyes on the ferry—The ferry that is usually designated for full-time spring breakers and parrot heads.

My aunt and uncle live in Port Clinton, home to a cute little downtown, a few different ferry services, and the Annual New Year's Eve Walleye Drop. (Where they lower a 20ft fiberglass fish by crane—a truly beautiful sight to behold.) Lucky enough for us, my aunt works part-time selling tickets for one of the ferries and I thought, if we ever had a chance at pitching the concept of putting a casket on a boat, this would be it.

So, we call her up.

"No way."

"C'mon!" I reply. "You could pull some strings."

She laughs. "I don't have that kind of pull. I take tickets, dude, and part-time at that!"

"Come on! There's not even going to be a body in the casket. It's just a box."

"Does it look like a coffin?"

"Kind of," I reply.

"How much does it look like a coffin?"

“It looks a lot like a coffin,” I admit, laughing.

“‘Cause it’s a coffin?”

“Yeah. But it’s an empty coffin.”

“No way, dude,” she says, laughing. “Even if I push it through as cargo, people are going to freak out if they see a coffin on the boat. That’s something the coast guard takes care of. People’d want to be having Jimmy Buffet-style pirate funerals all the time.”

“That’s awesome,” I say.

“You’d think so, but these people are crazy,” she says. “I wish I could be more help, but…” She pauses.

“Hey! You still there?” she asks.

“Yeah. Yeah,” I say.

“Can I call you right back? I think I have an idea,” she says. “You’re talking about sometime in April, right?”

“Right.”

“I’ll call you right back,” she says.

I wait impatiently. Assuming she’s going to call me back 30 seconds later. She doesn’t, but that’s okay.

The next day comes and I’ve accepted the fact that I need to start thinking about other options. I’m sure I know someone around here with a boating license, but around 3 pm, after

I've already reached out to a couple of characters who own jet skis, I get a text from my aunt

> Sorry for the delay. Here's the number of a guy your parents and I used to roll with. He works pretty closely with the guys who run the boats. He's a first mate of sorts. He'd be someone to talk to about getting your 'not coffin' on the boat. I'm sure your dad still keeps up with him. He's good about that.
>
> Rob with the Snake: 419-555-6492

Unreal. Uncle Rob works on the ferry.

I call him up.

"This Rob!" he answers.

"Hey Rob! This is Mic Fox. You probably don't remember me, but I'm Jim Fox's son and..."

"Holy shit. Michael Fox? How the hell are ya?" he asks excitedly.

I laugh. "I'm good, man! How're you doin'?"

"I'm good, man. Hey...if this is one of those weird calls about me doing something weird when you were a kid, know that

I never intended to do anything weird *around* you guys or *to* you guys or anything like that."

"What?" I say. "What? No? What do you mean? No."

"Nothing, nothing," he says. "I just…when I get phone calls from people I haven't seen in a while, where sometimes they say that I…or…when I was younger…and things were different back then you know…but that's no excuse…but I don't remember it the way they said…necessarily…"

"What? No," I say. "This isn't one of *those* calls."

"Sweet. That's great, man," he says. "So how are ya? What can I do for a man such as yourself? You are a grown man now, right? How old are you? You gotta be like 60, I dunno…61 years old. I dunno…maybe 62, 63, I dunno…64 years old. Right? Like, you have grandkids and stuff by now. Right?"

I laugh. "What? Are you serious? No. I'm not 60. How old are *you?* How could I be 60? You're not even 60. How could I be older than you?"

"I don't know, man. Time moves in mysterious ways."

"Not really. Rob, I hear you're workin' on the ferry now."

"Yessir," he says. "Captain Rob at your service."

"You're a captain?" I ask, surprised.

He laughs. "No, of course not, but they do let me try and park the boat sometimes. They call me Captain Rob because they know I like it. It's like when dentists call themselves

'Dr. Dentist' or whatever. They're not really doctors, but people call them that because they like it."

I laugh. "That's not *why* people call them doctors."

"Sure, it is," he says. "Trust me. I'm a doctor."

"That's insane," I say.

"Sure. Sure..." he responds. "So, what can I do for you?"

"Rob, this may sound like a weird request...but I'm trying to get an empty coffin from Port Clinton to Put-in-Bay, and my aunt told me that you worked on the boat, and..."

"No problem," he says, cutting me off.

"Really?"

"Sure man! No problem. As long as I tell them it's *empty*, it's no big deal." He says, emphasizing the word "empty" with finger quotes that stretch through the phone.

I laugh. "It *is* empty. Like, actually empty. I can explain..."

"The less I know, the better, my friend," he replies. "I don't care if there's a body. I don't care if you're moving product between here and Canada. The less I know, the better. We do stuff like this all the time."

"What? What do you mean?" I ask, regretfully—knowing, full well that, like Rob, the less I know, the better.

"You're family, man. We can always do weird stuff for family. Your parents have always been good to me. The least

I can do is help their 60-year-old son move some drugs and a body across the border," he says sweetly.

"Rob! Listen to me. There are no drugs. There is no body."

"Of course," he says. "Nothing to see here. I don't even know what you're talking about. Just text me the date and time you want to get this done and we'll make it happen."

"Thanks, Rob! I appreciate all the help. We'll be in touch."

And just like that, we've got the beginnings of a lovely funeral on our hands.

An Explanation

I probably need to address what's going on. Sorry if there's been some confusion or plot holes up to this point.

You're probably concerned as to why people are so gleeful and eager to make funny conversation about the death of a friend and a corresponding funeral. Yes—we're having a funeral for our dear friend, Arthur Fischer a.k.a. Fish a.k.a. Arthur McFischerson a.k.a. Swimmer a.k.a. Schwimmer a.k.a. David Schwimmerson a.k.a. Ross from *Friends*.

Fish is the keystone of an architecturally stout group of dysfunctional friends that grew up in Northwest Ohio. He is the glue that connects a group of people that, under any other circumstance, wouldn't associate at all, let alone keep in touch some 15 or 20 years after graduating (or not graduating) from high school. He is well-liked by most, despite his eccentricities, and is the type of person who's never met a stranger even if he wishes sometimes that he could. He's a friend to weirdos and normies, has-beens and townies, basement dwellers, and mothers at the PTO. He's got a memory like a steel trap and can recall someone's name and the place where he met them 20 years earlier (similar to that of Tammie Thompson, but with slightly better judgment). He's been like this since we were kids and can't turn it off, despite his better judgement and the weight that comes with remembering every stupid thing that every stupid person he's ever met has ever done.

Upon hearing of the death of our dear friend, many of us were heartbroken. And by many of us, I mean just our friend

Dave, because the rest of us (including Fish's family) were very well aware that Fish was *not* dead, and all of this was the most elaborate stunt that any one of us could have ever hoped to bring to reality.

"Why attempt to pull something so cruel and potentially harmful?" you ask.

To which I reply, "Well…it's a long story."

"But is it really?" you ask. "It sounds like run-of-the-mill trash behavior to me."

"Trash behavior?" I say, flabbergastedly. "What the hell is '*trash* behavior?' Who talks like that?"

"Trash behavior. You know, behavior like trash. Like, it seems like you and your friends are going out of your way to be cruel to your friend, Dave. Is it really worth all the trouble? And why does Dave deserve this? Why does he need to be at the end of this garbage stick?"

"Garbage stick?" I reply. "What the hell's a 'garbage stick?' And yes, it's totally worth it. Look, here's the deal…"

Our friend Dave, after moving to Kentucky and then back to Ohio and then to Tennessee and then to California and then to Oregon and then back to Tennessee and then back to California and then to Idaho for a second and then back to California, has decided that maybe it's time to settle down and get married to a nice young lady that puts up with all of his Daveness.

All of this is well and good. All of us are happy for Dave. Sure, some people lost some bets on whether or not he'd settle down before he turned 50, but we're happy regardless. We honestly thought he'd never meet someone who would voluntarily, legally attach themselves to our good man. But we're happy for him. She calls him on his bullshit. She holds him accountable. But she's sweet to him, and she can roll with the crew. She's a homie. She's solid gold. She's head and heels above any of the ladies that Dave has dated in the past.

It's what you want for your friend. It's what you want for everybody. Love is a rare thing these days. But our friend Dave has found it.

And we're stoked for him.

So, they got engaged this past fall. It was a very public, all-out, musical accompaniment-filled engagement, shot on multiple cameras and edited just so. It was pretty impressive, truth be told. Maybe too impressive. But they're in an impressive state of life. They've got some cheddar. They live in California. They're a couple of babes in their mid-to-late 30s. They're built for this. If they were any older, they'd be L.L.Bean models. If they were any younger, they'd be doing choreographed dances on some weird new app that I don't know about. But we're happy for them.

Then right around Christmas, a bunch of us get a letter (on stationery, no less) inviting us to Dave's bachelor party.

My Dearest Comrades,

I, your friend Dave, would like to cordially invite you to celebrate the last days of my life as a bachelor.

My lovely bride-to-be requests that we hold the bachelor festivities in the beautiful Napa Valley from the First through the Fifth of April.

Please make your reservations accordingly.

I look forward to seeing you and I hope you're well.

Best,

Dave

After receiving such a letter, the group text and chaos that ensues are obvious. But Fish, Doobs, Murphy, and I decide that we need to meet up and discuss it, as we're all back home for the holiday.

"Please make your reservations accordingly?!" says Doobs as we sit and wait for our food at Shoes. "What the fuck does that even mean?"

"You know what it means," says Murphy. "It means, we're paying our own way and we have no say in anything moving forward. This is who he is now. He's living a curated internet lifestyle and we're just side characters in the slow-motion, hazed-out version of his world. The dust settles beautifully. The sun glows through the trees. Everything is perfect. That's his new world. We're just living in it."

We all laugh. "This is just like him, though," I say. "One minute he's purchased enough speaker equipment to start his own festival. Then the next day he sells it all and he's committing to a 'minimalist skateboard-centric lifestyle,' whatever the fuck that means. Then he breaks his arm, quits skating, puts all his money in expensive jeans, and moves out to California. He ends up selling all of those clothes on consignment and falls in love with a chick from his past that happens to be working part-time at the consignment shop. It's like a bad movie, but updated day-to-day on the internet. He's an internet person, now. He's all in."

"You can't go halfway on the internet, Mic. You're either online or offline. He's an influencer. He influences," says Murphy.

"But I don't want to be ONLINE," says Doobs. "This is fuckin' bullshit. I will not be a part of his internet world. I will not be a pawn in his social media landscape. I refuse. And why the hell is his wife planning his bachelor party anyway? It's disgusting."

The table erupts with laughter and the sound of pint glasses.

"Easy, Doobs. Watch that blood pressure," says Murph. "You're right, though. That's the most disturbing part. It's pretty bold of her to acknowledge, *in writing*, the fact that she's planning his bachelor party. It seems out of character. I know we've only seen her a handful of times since we graduated, but she still seems chill. Is this a power play? Did she send out these invites? Does he even know about the bachelor party? I mean, that *is* his handwriting at the bottom of the letter. He must've read it. He must be okay with it, right? I'm with Doobs. I'm disturbed."

"We're all disturbed," says Fish. He's been sitting quietly, thinking, for the past few minutes. He pauses. Thinking. "We've got to do something."

"What do you mean?" asks Murphy, laughing excitedly. "I've got a really good, bad feeling about this."

We all laugh.

"He can't just throw his own bachelor party. And honestly, I don't think she forced his hand on this," says Fish. "You know Dave. Dave's always trying to blame his girlfriend for him wanting to do some dumb shit. Right? Like, remember the time he told us that Brianna chick was *making* him go to that Bigfoot convention? No one's girlfriend *makes* them go to a Bigfoot convention. It was just an excuse to get out of some other shit. And rather than telling us that he *wanted* to go to the Bigfoot convention, he decided that telling us his girlfriend was *making* him go to Bigfoot convention was more believable."

"Unreal," says Murph. "He's an artist."

"So *now*, I think he's trying to throw his own bachelor party in fucking wine country so he can take wild ass pictures of it for his internet people," says Fish.

"This will not stand!" cries Doobs.

"I think you're right," says Murphy. "If she typed up those invitations, there's no way she would have closed the letter with 'Please make your reservations accordingly.' That's so stupid. She would have a link to the hotel where she blocked some rooms off or something. But this thing has no direction at all. He wants *us* to plan his bachelor party, but he wants it to be in the *Napa Valley*. And he wants us to think that his future wife, his 'old ball and chain,' is forcing his hand on this."

"Right. Because the appropriate thing to do would be to let us plan his bachelor party," I say. "But he doesn't think he can trust us to throw him the photogenic, picture-perfect bachelor party that he wants to project to the world."

"So he's throwin' it himself like a freak!" says Doobs.

"Freaks!" says Fish.

We all pause for beer. Then Murphy breaks the silence.

"So…have we decided that we're not going to allow this fool to force us into throwing him a bachelor party in California wine country?"

"Yes," the three of us say in unison.

"The yesses have it!" exclaims Murphy, slamming his giant cup of wine on the table.[18]

"So, what the fuck are we going to do?" asks Doobs. "I say we go ahead with his plan—then none of us show up! That'll show him. That'll fuck his world up."

"Jesus," says Fish. "There's gotta be a real stupid way to pull something off. Something anyone else would see coming, but Dave would fall for without question."

"We could have him kidnapped," says Doobs.

"But that's so silly," says Murphy. "He'd figure it out. Plus, we'd have to go to California."

"Yeah, fuck that," says Fish. "How do we get him to come here?"

"Oh shit!" I exclaim. "We could have Johnny or someone pretend to get engaged and force him to come here for the 'wedding,' then *boom*-switcharoo, it's his bachelor party."

"That's cute," says Murphy.

---

[18] *Cup of Wine* is a Shoes specialty. It's a plastic, souvenir style, 32oz Cup (the kind you'd get at a baseball game) filled all the way to the top with boxed wine. It's intended to be shared, but I've never seen anyone do this.

"But he'd still want us to come out for his stupid thing. He'd want *two* bachelor parties, that selfish son of a bitch," says Doobs.

"Sorry," says Fish, "I'm still caught up on Mic saying 'boom-switcharoo.' Please don't speak like that in front of our friends."

"Oh, sorry bud. Didn't mean to grace your ears with such garbage talk," I say.

"You bet your ass you're sorry," he says. "You say 'boom-switcharoo' in front of me again and you won't see this face until it's lying face up in a casket."

Everyone laughs and pauses for beer.

Then pauses a little longer.

"Holy shit!" exclaims Doobs. "We're gonna kill Fischer."

—

So…no, we didn't decide to actually kill Fischer to ruin Dave's bachelor party—that's a little aggressive. But we did (after far too many drinks, mind you) decide to fake Fischer's death right before Dave's bachelor party. The idea being that Dave would have to cancel his overambitious and upsettingly under-planned bachelor party in order to attend the funeral of his dear friend.

Sure, there was probably an easier way to change up Dave's plans. We could call him out on his vague invitation and his new social media-filled lifestyle. We could've had a civil conversation and told him that we already had something planned for him.

Or we could elaborately fake the death of a friend, call in a bunch of favors, and spend a bunch of money that we don't have.

You tell me, which option sounds like the better time?

And sure, it's a lot of work. But anything worth doing in this life is worth the work. I'm sure someone's grandfather said that at some point.

And Northwest Ohio knows how to work. It's in our blood. This outrageous scheme may not pay well, but neither does the factory since they gutted the unions, so we might as well use our work ethic for a good time. If you don't flex that work ethic, you lose it. And that's something that I will not stand for. Hell, if you show the people of Northwest Ohio a good time, if you give them something to believe in, they're with you for the rest of their days.

So we decided to give them the rowdiest fake funeral they've ever seen. Sure, it's at the expense of our friend's bachelor party (and maybe his psyche), but that's a sacrifice we were willing to make. If you're going to do something, do something for the people. Give them hope. Give them an opportunity. Give them something to laugh about. Give them something to celebrate. They deserve that! *We* deserve that!

So, we called in some favors. We booked the wake at the bar and we booked transportation to the island via ferry for our water-front-phony-funeral.

We were feeling pretty good.

Tracy and Meghan started to talk about our plan with the regulars at Shoes. They said we should have a pretty good turnout for this thing. I figured that we'd have a funny little wake at the bar then a few friends and family would make it onto the ferry. I assumed once we got everybody off the ferry, we could pull the casket into town on some golf cart and have Fish be at some bar waiting for Dave. Then after Dave takes a couple of swings at him, we could spend the rest of the weekend laughing about how elaborate this whole thing was and give Dave a nice little bachelor party.

But things change.

Word started to spread amongst the townies beyond Shoes and in Fish's mother, Connie's, salon. Then, in February, I got an email from an old classmate via his law firm. I don't like getting letters from law firms. As legal ramifications terrify me. But alas:

Mr. Fox
Longtime, no see, my friend. Word has spread down here in Columbus that you and yours are throwing our friend, Arthur Fischer, a fake funeral on Put-in-Bay. Very Sick. My brother Travis and I would love to be of service if at all possible.

I've heard a rumor that Mr. Dubois and Mr. Murphy are organizing the wake at Shoes. If this is true, it is most excellent, and we look forward to being there.

I'm not sure if you have a location for the funeral service on the island yet, but if not, we would be happy to reach out to the National Parks as they oversee the grounds of Perry's Victory and International Peace Memorial to the War of 1812.

They don't usually perform fake funeral services on the grounds, but our great-grandfather was one of the historians involved in the construction of the monument in 1912. Along with his passion for post-revolutionary history, our great-grandfather had a passion for mischief. He was quite the elaborate prankster and prided himself on being able to talk his way out of any shenanigans that he and his buddies got themselves into.

After talking with our father and grandfather about continuing the legacy of our late great-grandfather, we thought that we would reach out to you, wondering if you'd like to perform your fake funeral service on the grounds of the monument.

Perry's Monument is the only international peace memorial in the national parks system. Our country and our world have been through a lot of heartache this past decade, and I can think of no better way to bring peace to these trying times than to throw an overly attended, overly elaborate, phony funeral for a friend.

I am confident that the Parks Service would grant our request, if you so choose.

No pressure, obviously.

Hope you're well. Glad to hear that you guys are still at it.

Regards,

Tyler Thompson

"Dammit. How are we supposed to pass that up?" asks Murphy [Murf], via video chat with way too many people—

a practice that our group of friends adopted early on, and has become a staple in work environments post COVID-19.

Also on the call:

[Doobs] Doobs,

[Fish] Fischer

[JW] Johnny Waterfall

[Pop] Michael Popper a.k.a. Pop

[Ging] Ginger, the Crawfish King of Columbus (a friend who did his college years in Louisiana and now speaks with the strangest accent you've ever heard)

[JJ] Josh Jameson a.k.a. Joshua Joshua a.k.a. Josh-Josh

and

[Mic] Myself

...

Pop: I don't think we should be fuckin' around with the Thompsons, bro.

JW: The fuckin' *Thompson Twins*. That's so ridiculous.

Mic: But guys, it would take it to the *next level*.

Doobs: You're gonna fuck this up, Mic. The Thompsons are trouble.

Pop: Seriously, dude. Like…I'm pretty sure that law firm they work for hid all that money for their parents. You don't want to get into bed with these people.

JJ: Yeah, man. You don't want to sleep with the Thompson twins.

Mic: What? We're not getting into bed with them. They just saw an excuse to reach out and thought this would make the funeral crazier.

JJ: Just don't get into bed with them.

Pop: Shut up, Josh-Josh. No one's talking about *sleeping* with the Thompson twins.

JW: [singing] I have a picture…

Pop: All I'm saying is that it complicates things. Getting these fools involved will not end well.

Ging: Pop's right, man. It's just going to make it more complicated. This is already over the top. It's a fake funeral for Chrissake.

JW: [singing] pinned to my *wall*...

Mic: That's what I'm saying! It's a *fake funeral!* If we're going to go for it, let's fucking go for it.

JW: [singing and mumbling] An image of something and something and laughing and something *it all!*

JJ: Yeah! Let's fucking go for it.

Doobs: Shut the fuck up, Joshua. The adults are speaking.

Murf: Cool it, Doobs. I don't know, man. It seems risky. We're talking about getting the National Parks involved. What if one of these fools goes rogue? What if someone lights the damn monument on fire? Are we liable for this shit?

JW: [singing] But look at our life now ...

Mic: [laughing] Guys, there won't be a fire. Funerals are very tame. We can control all this stuff. People can save the crazy until we get to the bars. Put-in-Bay has seen far crazier.

Pop: You're crazy. This is a horrible idea.

JW: [singing] All tattered and torn!

Ging: Mic's right, though. There's fools driving around that island in golf carts with puke on themselves. This is mild compared to that.

Fish: I don't know. I see the risk, but I can't imagine things getting that wild *at* the funeral. I'd think the wake would be more dramatic. It's at a bar. If people are going to get sloppy, I think it'd be there, not at the funeral itself.

Mic: Exactly. I think the setting would make it more legitimate.

JW: [singing] We fuss and we fight and delight in the tears that we cry *until dawn!*

Pop: What the fuck is Johnny talking about. Are you singing?!

Ging: Yeah bro—he's been singin' that fuckin Thompson Twins song this whole time.

JJ: You don't want to get in bed with the Thompson twins.

Pop: Jesus. It's *your* funeral, Fish.

[Everyone laughs]

JJ: Yeah, it's your funeral, Fish.

Doobs: Boooo...You disgust me.

Ging: I'm inspired, guys. I'm stoked.

JW: [singing] Hold. Me. Now. *Ohh*... Warm. My. Heart. Ohhhh, *stay with me!*

Everyone else via out-of-sync video chat:

Stay with me! Mumble start mumble start something start something start.

–

Then, around St Patrick's Day, my mother texts me a link to the online edition of our local paper, *The Citizen*. I'm hit with a paywall—which I understand the need for, but dammit, I hate a paywall. Assuming this is just a link to some offensive shit they printed in the "Opinions" section of the paper, I just text her back the word,

Paywall?

Instead of her calling me to read me the offensive shit that some ignorant bastard wrote about how "the rainbow doesn't belong to the gays" or "why am I not allowed to say *all lives matter?"* or some shit, she just texts me back a photo of a physical newspaper and the words,

Worth the paywall.

I click on the photo and zoom in on an article that my mother has circled with a highlighter.

Local Man Plans Parade for Friend's Phony Funeral

Oh, shit.

I call my mother. Evidently, our man, Ginger the Crawdad King of Columbus, decided to file some paperwork with the city requesting road closures for a New Orleans-style funeral procession.

Naturally, the gang gets on another video call…

Pop: What the fuck is wrong with you, Ginger?

Murf: Personally, guys, I just want to go on the record and say I am thrilled by all of this.

Ging: I told you guys I was inspired.

JW: This is so awesome.

Doobs: You guys are out of your goddamn minds. First, the fuckin Thompsons get involved and now we're throwing a fucking parade! We are playing with fire, my friends.

Fish: Yeah, guys. This seems like too much. I might be out on all this.

Mic: Hold your horses, boys. Hold your horses.

Ging: Yeah. You guys relax.

Mic: What's the story, Ginge?

Ging: So…I went down to the permit office last time I was in town.

JJ: As we all do.

Ging: Shut up, Josh-Josh. I went down there to see what I had to do to have a funeral procession. Like, a normal funeral procession, where all the cars get little flags and shit. Big car. Hearse. All that. And these two nice ladies said we didn't need a permit for it. But you can request a police escort if you'd like. So, I asked if the police bring the hearse with the escort...

Pop: Jesus Christ.

Ging: ...and they said that the funeral home would probably have a hearse as a part of their funeral package. And I told them that we weren't planning on using a funeral home. And they asked me what I meant.

Murf: I am thrilled.

Ging: I told them that it wasn't a real funeral. Just a fake funeral but we wanted it to seem real. And that I wanted there to be a marching band and stuff. And they told me that it sounded like a parade instead of a funeral. And I told them about living in Louisiana and how they do funerals down there, and...

Fish: This is insane.

Ging: ... they told me that I couldn't just throw a parade for no reason like you can in New Orleans. And then I said, it's not a parade, it's a fake funeral. And the one lady asked, "for who?" And I said, "for my buddy, Fischer." And the other lady asked, "Fischer who?" And I said "Arthur Fischer." And the First Lady asked, "Connie's son?" And I said, "Yeah! Connie's son." And the second lady said, "Oh! Connie was telling me about this the other day when I was getting my roots done. You guys are throwing a fake funeral to mess with a friend of yours, right?" And I said, in my most charming southern voice, "Yes ma'am, and if I may, you don't look old enough to be getting your roots done. Shoot, you don't look a day over twenty-nine." And she blushed and said, "You stop." And I said, "I would if I could, ma'am." And before you know it, people were making phone calls and people were throwing stamps around and people were filing paperwork, and just like that, we got a permit for a fucking parade.

Fish: Holy shit. That's crazy.

JJ: That's so great, Ginger. Way to persevere.

Mic: That's a ridiculous story. So, what do we need to do now?

Ging: I don't know. I did my part.

JW: Awesome.

Murf: Am I the only one who actually read the article?

[Silence]

Murf: C'mon, guys. The article laid it out. The city got the PTA and the high school band involved. They're holding a float contest during the funeral parade as a fundraiser for the new elementary school and shit.

JJ: We gotta do a float, guys!

Pop: You go ahead, Josh-Josh. The rest of us are going to try and *throw a fake funeral and a parade without Dave finding out.*

JW: That's a good point. How *doesn't* Dave already know?

Murf: Well, the article was pretty nonspecific. It didn't mention Connie or Fish or anybody. Dave definitely doesn't read the paper from his hometown, and even if he did, he's not really one to put two and two together.

Pop: Yeah. This is the fool who thought we had a psychic connection because he kept butt-dialing me.

JW: That's right! He called it something weird, right?

Murf: "Mind-link." He kept saying, "Popper and I have mind-link."

Ging: That's insane.

Murf: I'm not really all that worried about him finding out. I'm worried about how we're going to let him know that this whole thing was a ruse without him losing his damn mind.

Ging: That's a project for a different day.

JJ: Yeah—we've got a float to work on.

Doobs: Unbelievable.

Come late March, we realized that one of us was going to have to make the call—the call to Dave to tell him that Fish had passed away.

We hadn't yet decided how Fish was going to imaginarily die. It couldn't be too dramatic, as that could push Dave into an irretrievable state—or worse yet, he'd be driven to investigate.

So, we decided to be as vague as possible. We debated for days about who would be the most convincing in giving Dave the devastating news. We thought about asking Fischer's mother. But there's no way she could handle hearing a grown man cry on the other end of the phone without breaking down and blowing the whole thing to pieces. We weighed the pros and cons of each one of us. In the end, we landed on the only person we know whose naivety and childlike sense of wonder even come close to that of Dave's...

Our sweet, sweet Joshua Joshua.

Joshua Jameson a.k.a. Josh-Josh, would, from an outsider's perspective, appear to be a simple man. He works with his uncle building trailers just outside of town. His family has worked in industrial agriculture since the word "industrial" was able to be added in front of the word "agriculture." To a West Coaster or a New England old money monster, Dave and his family look like your run-of-the-mill Midwestern farm type. You'd assume they were simpletons as quickly as you'd imagine a Confederate flag bumper sticker on the back of one of their rusted-out trucks (despite the fact that this part of Ohio is far closer to the Canadian border than anything you could even remotely call the South.) But if you peel back that rust, you'll be pleasantly surprised to see a much deeper sense of societal understanding and empathy. Josh-Josh and his family are a part of what I'd call the Farm Fresh Socialists—a political ideology that is thought to be extinct in this part of the country.

Joshua's great-great-grandfather was an agricultural savant, a boisterous public speaker, and an organizer in the village of Yellow Springs, Ohio. As a follower of the teachings of Robert Owen, Josh's grandparents managed the entirety of their small utopian community's food production. While other members of this experimental community tried their hand at various small-scale crafts and jobs, the Jamesons were the steady force in keeping the community grounded, despite the occasional ego flare-ups that come with European immigrants who are new to socialism.

The Yellow Springs Jamesons moved further and further outside of town as time went on, acquiring land as they went. By the time the Civil War hit, the Jamesons had given away or sold all but five acres of their property to formerly enslaved families. They stayed in the Yellow Springs area, teaching sustainable farming techniques and philosophy until the Red Scare of the 1950s sent anyone with communist sympathies into hiding. While Josh-Josh's dad doesn't say much, he says just enough to let you know that he believes what he believes, he lives out those beliefs, and he's seen some shit.

Josh's mother is from our hometown. She met Josh's dad while she was waiting tables at Shoes. The way she tells the story:

> "I was working my way through school at the bar and this big handsome farmer

> type walks in with a guy named John that I knew from around. We get farmer types a lot, but I hadn't seen this guy around before. I know John always drinks Blatz, so I brought two beers over to the table and said, 'Hey, John. Who's your friend?' Something I would never do. That's so bold. Then John said, 'Hey Joan! This is Joe Jameson,' and I just thought that was the coolest name I'd ever heard. Then he said, 'Pleasure to meet you, Joan. I'm Joe.' I thought, 'No one's ever said *'Pleasure to meet you, Joan'* to me in my whole life!' So I say to myself, 'Holy shit. I'm going to marry this guy.' But I didn't say it to myself. I said it out loud. To him. Then he laughed and said, 'I could be so lucky,' and I fainted. I fell out. Can you believe that?"

So yeah, Josh's mother is a ham. And while Josh's dad is a quiet man, don't mistake this stoic nature for simplemindedness. His four sons and two daughters, Jacob, Jeromy, Jonah, Jinelle, Joanna, and Josh-Josh, are some of the most well-read, hard-working, sneaky-ass fools in the game.

Joshua's oldest two brothers are both tenured professors. His sisters, Jinelle and Joanna, run the local farmers co-op and both have lovely families of their own. Jonah runs the farm with his dad, and Josh-Josh works with his mother's brother building trailers for people. Custom trailers. Very expensive trailers. But he would never say that. He'd say, "I build trailers with my uncle." He doesn't care about money or prestige or any of that. He likes living out in the country. He leans into it. And you'd better believe he hams it up, just like his mother, for anybody that would assume he's some country bumpkin—including our friend Dave.

Dave is the opposite of Joshua. He wants people to think he's doing well. He *needs* people to know that he's not some Midwestern cornstalk, and while the rest of us know that Josh-Josh leans into his country-ass persona, Dave thinks that's who Joshua is. He's always saying stuff like, "Josh-Josh, you're smart. Why are you still building trailers for your uncle? You could do anything. You're a bright guy. You just gotta find something that fits you. You should go to college, man. Best years of my life."

Anyone else would be offended by someone speaking that way to them, let alone someone like Dave, but Josh-Josh thinks it's hilarious. He doesn't tell Dave that his uncle works for *him* and that his "trailer" business isn't some utility trailer welding shop, but a full-blown custom fabrication operation that sells internationally. Instead, he just says, "I don't know, Dave. I'll figure it out one of these days, I guess."

So, when we settled on Josh to give Dave the sad news, he was tickled. None of us were listening in on the call, but Josh-Josh graciously recorded the whole thing on his answering machine at work and sent it to all of us without any context.

"*Josh-Josh-Josh-Josh*! What's up, man! Long time no see! How's it hangin'? You getting ready for the big bachelor weekend? I haven't heard any plaaayy-onnns yet, so I assume you guys have quite the surprise in store! Sweet baby K said no strippers. But I know you guys are going to try to get stripperrrrrs! But seriously, don't. She'll be so pissed. But probably not because she's chill. Dude! I'm so pumped."

"Hey Dave. Great to hear your voice man. Where you at right now?"

"Californiaaaa babe! You know what it is!"

"I know where you live. Are you at home? In the car? What?"

"I'm at home, chillin'. Why? It's only 5:30 bro. How late is it there? Is it, like, 8:30? Is it dark?"

"Yeah. It's dark."

"That's so crazy man. It's like not even close to dark here, bro."

"Dave. I need you to sit down."

"Yo…you OK, Josh-Josh? You're putting off negative vibes."

"Dave. Fischer passed away this afternoon."

Silence.

"What? Repeat that. I think I misheard you."

"Fischer passed away this afternoon."

(At this point you can hear Josh-Josh actually get choked up, because he's actually realizing what it's like to tell someone that their friend died.)

Silence.

“What do you mean? What happened.”

(At this point, Josh-Josh realizes that it hasn’t quite hit Dave yet, but it’s about to. He also realizes that he didn’t plan this out at all and he doesn’t have a story to tell Dave about how Fish died.)

“I mean he died, Dave. Fish died.”

(At this point. Josh-Josh starts crying, and Dave starts crying, and truthfully, it’s a pretty emotional phone call to listen to.)

“I know what you said, Joshua. But how did he die? What happened?”

“Natural causes,” says Josh.

“What?”

“Natural causes. He died peacefully in his sleep.”

(At this point you hear a big yelping noise from Josh-Josh followed by him muting his phone. This is because the tears of sadness, have turned into tears of uncontrollable laughter. He realizes that he’s going to have to explain how a 35-year-old man dies “of natural causes, peacefully in his sleep.” He regains his composure after, again, realizing that this whole thing is very dark.)

“What do you mean by ‘natural causes?’ He’s, like, 35 years old. Thirty-five-year-olds don’t just ‘die of natural causes.’”

“I don’t know what to tell you, man.”

Silence.

"I'm so sorry, man. We're all torn up about it," continues Joshua.

"Why now? Like...why before..." says Dave, holding back tears. Stuttering, thinking.

"Why'd it have to be before the bachelor party," Dave says.

Silence.

"What do you mean?" asks Joshua.

"I mean...uh...this is so selfish of me to think like this... but I really wanted Fish to be at the bachelor party. I wanted the whole gang to be there. It's not going to be the same without him."

"Dave. Fish just died. Are you honestly thinking about the bachelor party?" asks Joshua, certain that Dave's just flailing, processing. He's a selfish guy, but not like this.

"Well... how can I not? The party's this weekend. And y'all have spent all this time planning all these surprises and everything, and now Fish isn't going to be there. It's just not going to be the same."

"Dave...the funeral is this weekend. No one's going to your bachelor party. Including you."

"What do you mean?! It's *my* bachelor party! I *have* to go to *my* bachelor party," Dave says, crying.

"*There is no bachelor party, Dave.* Fish's funeral is this weekend and we're all going to that instead. *Obviously*."

"But what about all the surprises?!" cries Dave.

"What are you talking about?!" screams Josh-Josh. Now he's upset.

Silence.

"Dave…Fischer's funeral is this weekend. I will keep you posted on where and when. Forget about the bachelor party. That's not what's important right now. We need to be there for Fish and his family. We *are* his family."

"You're right. We can reschedule the party…sorry…this is just a lot to process…I really wanted Fish to be there.

"I know. Me too, buddy. I'm sorry. Love you, bud. We'll be in touch."

—

Upon hearing a conversation like this, a few emotions rise to the surface, but luckily for us, we have the poetic sensibilities of our good friend Daniel "Double-Dip" DuBoise to describe the feelings at hand.

"That motherfucker. So, you're telling me that you called this loser to tell him that one of his best friends has just died, and he ends up crying because no one's coming to his bachelor party? I don't want to see this asshole ever again. But when I *do* see him, I think the whole lot of you are going to have to pull me off of his bloody corpse. This fool's the one who's gonna end up in that casket. That fucking loser. And you told him that Fish died of 'natural causes?' That about gave me a damn heart attack. Then that stupid idiot just lets that detail slide? Jesus Christ. Somebody put him down."

"Damn, Doobs. Tell us how you really feel," says Murphy.

But honestly, all of us were a little hot. How are you supposed to react to something like that? It's the most selfish reaction Dave could've had in that situation. It's so upsetting, but after the dust settles, you realize that maybe it's for the best.

A long con involving the stress and heartache of the passing of a friend is a horrible thing to put on someone. We were all feeling guilty about it. But...

If...in that moment of distress, instead of thinking of his friend or the pain his friend's family must be going through, that someone reacts in such a selfish and self-centered way, then I say *all bets are off*.

Suddenly, all of our collective guilt evaporates. The plan has taken a new shape. We started off thinking this would be a lofty ploy and excuse to give Dave a brutally sadistic bachelor party. But now we find ourselves looking at it from a different angle. We're going to run Dave through the wringer. We're going to give it our all. Fish's funeral a.k.a. Dave's bachelor party is going to be an all-out suffer fest. We're set on emotionally destroying him.[19]

---

[19] See how that anger progressed so rapidly? So aggressive. But that's what I was talking about earlier. If you feel like someone's disrespecting your people—disrespecting your fallen comrades—then, for whatever

As the group trades takes on the nuances of Dave's selfishness and stupidity, we eventually cool off. (And thank God, because Doobs was getting way too heated. It's not good for his blood pressure.) This would be our last video conference before the funeral. We needed to make sure everyone's on the same page.

Murphy was kind enough to send out an electric, editable, color-coordinated spreadsheet complete with a schedule of daily activities and everyone's responsibilities throughout the weekend.[20]

Everything was pretty well planned out. We had coordinated with the city regarding the parade. They told us that the mayor thinks it's hilarious. She's a sick son of a bitch, but whatever works.

Most of us who don't live in town were getting in on March 31st. According to Josh-Josh, Dave was planning on flying in the following morning and heading straight to the wake. The parade is supposed to start at Shoes and do a loop: down a few blocks of Main Street, down past the elementary school, and back to the bar—maybe 15 blocks total. That's longer than I'd like, but we take what we can get.

When the parade ends back at Shoes, any little crowd we would've picked up along the parade route will disperse and

---

reason, you may find it necessary to burn down their house, if only metaphorically.

[20] The initiative everyone has shown through this process is very impressive. Think: if we could collectively aim this brainpower at a good cause rather than at the emotional destruction of a friend, we could change the world. But alas.

we'll make our way up to Put-in-Bay. Uncle Rob told me to call him once we were on our way so he could give the boat crew a heads up on what was going down.

Once we're off the ferry, I figure we'll just rent a golf cart and drive the casket over to the monument for the funeral. The Thompsons assured us that everything would be fine and they had everything "all set up." And while I don't believe them for a second, we can always improvise if we get stopped by some park police.

Everything after that is up in the air; but that's fine, right?

Right?

As everyone looked through their spreadsheets, Popper was going off about how we needed to figure out how Fish was going to show up out of the blue without Dave throwing a fit.

"Look! All I'm saying is that I don't see how you idiots think it's okay to go in without a plan as to how Fish is going to just show up out of the blue without Dave throwing a fit. After all this planning—throwing a fucking parade, secretly getting a coffin on a boat, and letting the fucking Thompson twins help us throw a funeral in the middle of the lake, you freaks think it's just no big deal to improvise the grand finale!"

"The fucking *Thompson Twins*. It gets me every time," says Johnny.

"This isn't the fucking saxophone! This isn't a fucking drum solo. You can't just impro—"

Popper is stopped in his tracks, looking at his phone. Everyone looks up from their spreadsheets.

Silence.

"You ok, Pop? What's up?" asks Ginger.

More silence.

"Pop!"

"Sorry guys. I..."

"What is it?" asks Johnny

"It's Kelsey."

"Kelsey...like...Kelsey Kelsey?" asks Ginger.

"Yeah," says Popper, just barely shaking his head.

"What'd she say?" asks Johnny.

All of the sudden, everyone simultaneously receives a screen shot of Popper's phone:

Kelsey

Hey Pop. I want in.

Doobs breaks the silence.

"What the fuck does this mean?"

"It means she knows," says Pop.

"This is so upsetting," says Murphy.

"Knows what?" asks Johnny.

"She knows what we're doing," says Pop.

"What? No way," says Ginger.

"Of course, she does," says Josh-Josh. "I messed up."

"*What?!* You told her, Joshua?! What is wrong with you?!" demands Doobs.

"No, no, of course not, but I told Dave that Fish died of 'natural causes.' You don't think she asked him how Fish died? You don't think she knows that that's incredibly stupid?" explains Josh-Josh.

"Of course, but you didn't tell *her*. You told Dave, and Dave *is* stupid," says Ginger.

"Right, but she knows us, man," says Josh-Josh. "I thought of it as soon as it left my mouth. Like, 'Joshua, you idiot, Kelsey's going to know that's bullshit.' If she was just some random chick that Dave met out in California, that'd be one thing. But she's not. I mean, shit! She was *with* Popper during at least one of those butt-dial/mind-link incidents. She knows what we're capable of. She knows how gullible

Dave is. She knows we bait him. She *fucking* knows. Sorry guys. I let the team down."

"No, you didn't, Joshua. You hold your head up high," says Murphy.

"But what the fuck *does* that mean?" asks Johnny. "She wants *'in?'* *p*What does that mean?"

"It means she wants in on the bit," says Pop. "She's too damn smart. Why the fuck is she with Dave?"

Awkward silence.

"It doesn't matter. They love each other. She thinks he's funny—and he is. He's stupid, but he's funny. This is a family. *This* is a family dynamic. If we can make it through this, it may push us to the other side of all this awkwardness," I say.

"So, we have to let her in?" asks Ginger.

"We have to let her in," says Popper. "If we don't, who knows what'll happen. She could fuck with us all weekend. Hell, she could tell Dave the whole thing's a sham!"

"She wouldn't do that," I say. "She respects the bit too much. If she hasn't floated that idea to him already, then she just wants in on the bit. Like old times."

"Dammit. I'm so stressed," says Doobs.

"Not worth the stress Doobs. Eat a gummy. We're going to need your energy this weekend," says Murphy.

"What do we do? We just see what she has in mind? We can't just adjust the whole plan to deal with this," says Fischer.

Silence.

"Yo, Pop… What do you think she has in mind?" asks Josh-Josh.

"God…I don't know, but I bet it's pretty wild."

—

So, if you didn't catch that, Kelsey is Dave's fiancé. Though Kelsey and Dave didn't date until Dave moved out to California for the second time, they'd known each other for much longer. Kelsey grew up with all of us. We saw her almost every day for the majority of our adolescent years. We did everything together. She was as much a part of the crew as any of us. It was a big squad. And she was our queen bee. She didn't have many girlfriends through those years and could go toe to toe with any one of the fools on our team. She could hold her own. You have to be able to do that if you're going to hang with a bunch of teenage boys. We were awestruck by her confidence and her ability to talk shit better than anyone. Teenage boys are sloppy with their confrontations, figuring things out on the spot, but Kelsey grew up with three older brothers and could destroy anyone that came close to disrespecting her or treating her like a silly little teenage girl. She didn't take shit from anyone…

…except for Popper.

She loved Popper, and Popper loved her. They played a decades-long game of chess where their ability to pick at each other's insecurities opened up holes for real conversation. They explored each other's fears and vulnerabilities. They were smart. While the rest of us fumbled our words and picked at our pimples, Kelsey and Popper bounced ideas and struggles and life off each other. If any of us ever stepped to one of them, the other was there to put us in our place. They were a unit, arm in arm. Best buds. Obsessed with each other.

But as we got later into high school, the crew started to have less time together. People got busy. We'd see each other on the weekends, but on the day-to-day, it was just quick chats in the halls between classes. But not Pop and Kelsey. They were as close as two people could be. They had mad love for each other, but adolescent influence makes people behave very strangely.

If there was ever a function, the two of them were always too cool for school. If there was a football game, they were under the bleachers getting stoned. If there was a school dance, they were on the roof of the gym drinking warm beers. They were living a pretty romantic, counter-culture, John Hughesian lifestyle. And they seemed to love it.

But we all know how this story ends.

No one knows exactly what happened, but we all know that it sucks. They were having a deep conversation the way only teenagers do—where any remotely abstract concept that drifts into your mind carries the weight of the entire universe. Then the one tried to kiss the other and someone pushed someone away and said "I love you, and we're friends, but I don't feel that way about you," and the other one got hurt. They decided they needed to re-evaluate their friendship. They kept trying to make it work, but the tension always sent one of them into a crazy place where only love-struck teenagers exist, and before you know it, they're both at our senior prom, separately. Popper's date, the antithesis of Kelsey. And Kelsey's date, the antithesis of Popper.

You hate to see it, but it writes itself. We all hung out that summer before people went off to college. Tensions seemed to be settling. Kelsey went out west to work on some weird commune-y, co-op, live-work farm situation, and Popper went to college outside of Dayton to study finance.

They kept in touch here and there, but people get busy, and who knows how long it's been.

Kelsey hollers at us here and there, but she's got a whole other life three time zones away, and she's had that other life for 17 years now. I'm proud of her. She's paved her own way.

Pop graduated from school and moved to Boston to work for some firm. He hated Boston and moved to New York, the home of people who hate Boston. Then, right before the pandemic, Pop moved back to Ohio and got a gig working as a financial adviser for some company in Cleveland. I don't think he likes Cleveland either, but it feels closer to home than out east, and for better or worse, there's no place like home.

I think Pop and Kels will always have that love for each other, the way you do with your first real big love. They grew up together. They wouldn't be the people they are today if it weren't for each other.

But I know Popper still thinks about her. She's the one that got away. And she's awesome; it'd tear me up too.

When we found out that she and Dave connected randomly when he moved out west, we were all thrilled. It brought her back into our lives, and we missed her. I imagine it felt different for Pop.

Dave?

She's going to end up with Dave?

But Dave's an idiot!

Or maybe he's not. He's got her.

—

I talked to Pop a few times in the days leading up to the funeral. I wanted to know what kind of wrench Kelsey was trying to throw in the mix. I wanted to know if she *actually* knew what was going on, but all I got were crickets. Crickets or not, this funeral was going to happen.

Pop was going to need to be okay with seeing Kelsey…and visa versa.

We're all adults here. It's nice to see old friends. It's nice to reminisce. But things change, and people grow at different rates. Over this weekend, we were all going to need to be okay with that. To pull this off, we were all going to need to suppress the animalistic tendencies of falling into old roles. We were going to need to be adult versions of ourselves. Because this is an adult moment. It's a funeral, dammit, and we needed to act like it!

The night before the funeral, there was tension in the air. Not a bad vibe, just an energy. There were some texts here and there amongst the gang as everyone rambled into town. Under normal circumstances, a holiday or whatever reason a bunch of us were back home, we would've all met at the Horseshoe for beers. Instead, everyone hung with their families or sat at the hotel bar. It was quiet amongst us. No one spoke of the obvious anticipation that comes with organizing something like this. I imagine it feels like the lull before a big football game or the first performance of a play. Everyone knew what was about to happen, but felt like if we talked about it, we'd be jinxing ourselves. So everyone stayed in that evening, but you could slice the energy like butter.

My brother, traditionally a nocturnal character, sent me a photo around 11 pm of a banner hanging over the bridge downtown.

R.I.P. FISH GONE BUT NOT FORGOTTEN

"Duuuude...did you make that?" I asked him.

He responded around midnight. "Dawg...you have no idea how wild this is going to be."

And he was right. I did not.

SORRY 4 YOUR LOSS

You Can't Spell Funeral Without 'FUN'

Here we are. April 1st. April Fools' Day, mind you. We didn't plan it this way. But it's funny how things play out.

I finish up breakfast with my folks and get dressed for the visitation of our dear old friend, Arthur Fisher a.k.a. Fish a.k.a. Fisherman a.k.a. Fisher-Price a.k.a. Price Is Right.

I called Fish before breakfast to see how he was doing. For this day to go the way it should, it's very important that he isn't actually dead. It would be a huge bummer if we went through this whole fake funeral just to find out that he was actually in some sort of weird accident and died anyway. The joke would be on *us* at that point, and we can't have that. Not today.

"Listen, man, as long as you're safe and you stay away from Dave, I don't think it matters what you do," I say.

"But, like...should I go down there? I don't think I want to see people crying and shit. I know that they know that I'm not actually dead, but like...it's still weird. I don't want to see my mother at my own funeral. That's so dark."

"Right. You don't need to do anything you don't want to do, ya know. Like...you let us 'kill' you for the bit. What a gift."

He laughs. "It's so fucked up. You ever think about how fucked up it is? This is so overboard. Like...this may permanently mess up Dave's brain."

"'But what about *my bachelor party*?'" I say, mocking Dave's phone call with Josh-Josh.

He laughs. "Yeah, dude...I keep forgetting about that. Fuck this guy. He can handle it. I keep going back and forth. I want to be down there to see him during this."

"You just wanna watch the world burn?"

"Ha, no. But the wake sounds like it's going to be the fun part. I don't want to miss the fun part."

"This is messed up," I say. "No one should ever talk about how fun a wake is going to be."

"I know. But it's not real. And it's *my* wake."

"You're right. It's your party. You can cry if you want to."

"What's this fucking parade going to be like?"

"I have no fucking clue. I gotta call Doobs and see what the plan is. You just going to hang at mom's house until we head up to the lake?"

"I guess. I may pregame somewhere else. Maybe I'll go eat some breadsticks at the mall."

"That's the saddest shit I've ever heard. I didn't know the mall was still open."

“I asked my brother about it last night. He says there’s like six stores that just sell random amazon returns. There’s a semi-permanent Halloween store. The movie theater’s some weird church, now. And the Spencer’s Gifts is still there.”

“Damn. And the breadstick place?”

“The breadstick place is the only thing holding that mall together.”

“Man.”

“I bet the whole thing will be some huge weird indoor post-apocalyptic-themed paintball course by the end of the decade.”

“And that’s, like, best case scenario.”

“Yeah, that kinda sounds awesome.”

“It does. Weird mannequins and shit standing around. It’s like when Greg and Diego bought the old Chuck E. Cheese and tried to turn it into a live band animatronic karaoke bar.”

“Totally. Didn’t D go down to Florida or something and learn how to program those robots and shit?”

“Yes, dude. *That’s* a subculture. He said that old man who was teaching him about them robots kept asking him to sleep in his bed and shit.”

“That’s fucked up.”

“I know.”

“Whatever ended up happening with that?”

“Him and the old man?”

“No, the Chuck E. Cheese robot karaoke thing.”

“I think they got close to opening up. Then COVID hit, then the flood, and I think all the robots got fried.”

“Dammit! That’s horrible.”

“I know. So, you’re going to the mall to carb load. You just want us to call you when we know what the hell’s going on?”

“I guess,” he says somberly.

“Chin up, Fish. It’s your special day. You figure out how you’re going to let Dave know that you’re not dead?”

“No. Maybe I’ll just text him right now.”

“Motherfuckerrrr…”

“Relax dude. I’ll figure it out.”

“Love you, bud. Glad you’re not dead.”

“Me too. Keep me posted.”

—

As I start driving to Shoes, I’m overcome with actual emotion—not in the way you normally would while heading to a friend’s funeral, but in the way, I imagine a father feels walking his daughter down the aisle, in an “Oh shit…we’re actually doing this. Are we going to pull this off?" sort of way. I was shaking with nerves and excitement, the way Johnny Waterbottle was knowing that Dave wholeheartedly believed that my sister was the love child between my mother and a small Caribbean man.

A billion thoughts race through my head. I think about Fish. I think about Dave. I think about growing up with these weirdos and how none of them even gave this plan a real second thought. I think about this town and how despite the stupidity (and possible illegality) that comes with faking someone's death, the ladies at the planning office just fast-tracked a parade for us—for no real reason. Then I think about the fact that I don't actually have any real information on this parade or the funeral or anything at this point.

I texted Uncle Rob last night, making sure that we were still good to get this coffin onto the ferry. He didn't respond until this morning.

> Oh shit. Totally forgot. Just text me when you guys get into town and we'll figure it out.

I texted Murphy to see if I need to bring anything to Shoes. All he said was,

> Bring some tissues and a strong sense of self.

I texted Doobs to see if he'd had any details about the parade. He responded immediately with,

> Hey Mic, why dont you just fucking relax. I've got it under control. Put on your big boy pants, cuz DADDY'S GOT THIS.

Everyone seems to be cool with just improvising this whole thing. Under ordinary conditions, this would give me an anxiety attack, but these aren't ordinary conditions, these are *extraordinary* conditions.

I sit at a stoplight waiting to turn left. Ahead of me, my elementary school. Across the street from that, a little house that houses my childhood dentist's office. Beside that, an ice cream and chocolate shop—a local institution and the type of place that can only exist in a town like this. My mom would always take us for ice cream after we went to the dentist. I thought it was beautifully ironic, and I see, in this moment, that it probably shaped the angle that I take on life to this day.

I'm feeling very nostalgic. It's easy in a place like this. Despite the backwardness of some of its current political leanings, it's still great. It's people trying to do their best. Sure, there is some misguidedness, but that's true of any place. People go with what's in front of them. If you want people to do better things, then you've got to show up and put those better options in front of them, because around here, we don't have time to go out looking for other options. We're too busy just trying to make it work.

Today could just be another Friday in Northwest Ohio. But there's a better option today. Today's better option is attending the fake funeral for a dear old pal.

As I look at the dashboard and note the time, I think, "Oh, shit, I bet Dave and Kelsey just landed."

"Oh shit, I wonder if Kelsey actually knows what's going on."

"Oh shit, I wonder what kind of crazy shit she wants to pull if she *does* know."

And before I can go too far down the rabbit hole—wondering what a friend that we haven't seen in 15 years, who is currently engaged to our other friend who currently thinks that our *other* friend is dead, wants to do with the knowledge that the friend, who's supposedly dead, isn't *actually* dead—my eye is pulled to the street as I see five giant nautical-themed parade floats pass through the intersection.

My jaw drops and my eyes inflate. I look to my passenger seat as though someone's going to be there and instead, I make eye contact with the elderly woman in the car next to me. She rolls down her window and yells something.

I roll down my window and yell back at her, "Sorry, what?"

She yells again, "The parade's at noon! Lotta fish stuff! My hairdresser's son faked his own death! Gonna be a lot of fun! You gotta come!"

I laugh. "Yeah! Yeah, I heard about that. I'll see you there?"

"I bet you will, sugar lips." She winks at me and then blows me a kiss.

The light turns green and she drives away. I stall the car. "Did she call me 'sugar lips?'"

The large pick-up behind me honks and quickly pulls beside me. There are 6 teenagers in the truck with the windows down. The one driving the truck yells, "*Long live the Fishman*!" The rest of the car shouts in celebration. He flips me the bird and peels away, his dual exhaust engulfing my rental car.[21]

I am thrilled.

I turn left and see that the entrance to Shoes is blocked off. There are two police cars, an ambulance, and a fire truck with their lights on in the parking lot.

Dammit. Something happened. I don't like talking to police, but the odds of me knowing one of these cops from back in the day is pretty good (for better or worse), and Jesus, I guess I've got to figure out what's going on.

So, I slowly roll up to the entrance with my window down. One of the police officers notices and approaches my car. I recognize him, but don't know him. He graduated with one of my baby sisters. Even as a kid, he *looked* like a cop. He seems on edge—not what you want from a police officer. He keeps his distance. We're both waiting for the other to speak first.

I break the silence. "Sir! I was supposed to meet some friends here in a bit. Is everything all right?"

"You Fox?"

"Yes, sir."

---

[21] "Rolling Coal" is the practice of tweaking a diesel engine to emit large amounts of black sooty exhaust fumes from its tail pipe. It's currently prohibited in Maine, Utah, New Jersey, Maryland, Colorado, and Connecticut. Which makes sense. "But we ain't in Connecticut are we you dumb son of a bitch!" So…alas.

"I'm going to need you to turn off the vehicle and step out of the car."

I proverbially piss my pants. Cops stress me out.

"All right. May I ask why, sir?"

"Turn *off* the *vehicle* and *step out* of *the car.*"

I proverbially shit my pants.

"No problem."

I step out of the car. I am wearing all of my funeral attire aside from my jacket.

"Put your hands on the hood of the car and spread your legs, please."

Holy shit. Something horrible happened. We're fucked. I don't know how, but I knew that this day was not going to end well.

"Do you have anything in the vehicle that I need to know about? Any cooperation from you would be greatly appreciated," the officer says as he pats me down.

"No, sir. Just meeting some friends here. May I ask what's going on?" I ask, my voice quivering.

I rattle my brain. What the hell could this be about? Is faking someone's death illegal if it's only to mess with one stupid person? Probably. Did we draw too much attention to this whole thing? Did I get roped into something else by accident? Is Uncle Rob actually trying to use this coffin to move drugs to Canada? I thought Canada had enough drugs. I know he mentioned that on the phone, but I didn't think he was serious. Shit.

"You're being arrested for drug trafficking in international waters," he says, putting my hands behind my back.

"And for being a little bitch!" shouts a voice over the PA of the fire engine.

I turn and look at the cab of the truck. My cousins Brad and Chad are sitting in the fire truck, laughing their asses off.

The officer laughs and says, "Sorry man. Tell your sister I said 'hey.'"

"Tell her yourself," I retort. I try to recapture my breath. "I'm going to have to change my pants you *fucking monsters!"*

Brad and Chad get out of the truck and run at me. Big bear hugs all around.

"God. Sorry, player. That shit's too crazy. We couldn't not do it," says Chad.

"Yeah, man. If you did actually shit your pants, I've got two pair on right now. You could just have one of mine," says Brad.

"I'm good. I'll die younger, but I'm good," I say. "What the fuck are you guys doing here?"

Brad is a fire chief in Columbus. Chad is a big-dog EMT somewhere in the Carolinas. Their mother is my father's sister. They are objectively good people, but too funny for their own good. They're the guys you want showing up when shit hits the fan.

"Well, Mom was getting her hair cut, and her hairdresser told her that you assholes were faking your buddy's death to fuck with another one of your friends," explains Brad.

"She told us about it at dinner last night. We both just happened to be in town, visiting. So, I called up some buddies at the station here, and they said they already knew about it. Said you fools were throwing a parade. There ain't no parade without a fire engine, so here we are."

"Jesus. Here we are." I say.

"Well, dude…you gotta get in there," says Brad. "This wake isn't going to throw itself. We'll be around if you need us. I think they said the parade was going to start at noon?"

"Yeah…I honestly don't know anything about it. But I saw a few big floats on my way in."

"Ohhh yeah," says Chad. "We saw a bunch sitting in the lot across from the station. If y'all weren't planning on this being an ordeal, you might be in over your head. But we gotchu. Let us know what you need."

"Shit, OK. Love you guys."

"You too, bub."

I snake my way through the police cars and fire trucks and find a parking spot close to the building. The Horseshoe is only maybe half a mile from downtown, but the way it's situated makes it feel secluded.

The front of the building faces the street. From this direction, Shoes looks like any other small Midwestern brick building. The neon in the hazy window is the only giveaway that it is, in fact, a tavern. But during the day, when the light is off, it could be anything.

The back of the building faces a train track and a 10-acre patch of corn or beans, depending on the year. Ten acres is quite small for a cornfield, especially in this part of the country. It was originally a much bigger farm that got sold off during the industrial revolution, but for some reason, the owner at the time refused to sell those ten acres. In any event, the industrial revolution comes and goes, and here we are. Ten acres of corn in the middle of town.

The building was originally built as a hat factory in the late 1800s. The story of how the building got its horseshoe shape is debated. Some say the furnace in the middle of the building caught a bunch of straw hats on fire and sent the building into a blaze. Others say that the factory owner's wife caught him having an affair and set off a bunch of fireworks inside the building. Regardless of which story you believe, both stories end with the fire department getting to the scene, putting the fire out, leaving a hollowed-out shell of a building, the factory owner nowhere to be found.

The owner's wife, Miss Susanna, rebuilt the building, salvaging three of the four walls, and turned it into her home. She planted a garden in the middle of the building since the original roof and back wall had been blown out.

She spent the rest of her days sitting in a hammock in the middle of her garden, watching the train pass between her home and the cornfield on the other side of the tracks.

She never had any children of her own, so when she passed away she left the building to the 7-year-old son of the farmer who owned the cornfield on the other side of the tracks. That 7-year-old is Tracy's late father, Don—the founder of Shoes.

To this day, whenever the train goes by the Horseshoe, the whole bar toasts Miss Susanna for the greatest gift this town could ever receive. If one of the old heads, who's been sitting at the bar since before Tracy could walk, sees the train coming, he'll put a quarter in the jukebox and sing along to the song as loud as he can:

"*Oh, Susanna! Don't you cry for me! Somethin' somethin' somethin' somethin' with a banjo on my knee*!"

—

There are more cars in the parking lot than I'd assumed there'd be. Despite the unexpected welcome from the local police and my cousins, I still feel like I'm actually going to a real funeral. I've talked myself into it. People talk themselves into stuff all the time, and I try not to send myself down those paths, but here I am. I get myself together and enter through the screen door on the side of the building.

I open the door straight into Meghan.

"Mic! I mean…I'm *so glad* you were able to make it. How was the drive? I'm sure Connie will be *so glad* that you're here in this *difficult time*," she says, changing her tone from excited to comically somber.

"Oh, yes. How's she holding up?" I ask, over concernedly.

"She's taking it hard, as any mother would. She can't stop talking about it, honestly. I think the entire town is in on it at this point."

"Yeah…there's a fucking fire truck in the parking lot."

"You bet your ass there's a fire truck in the parking lot. I thought they were going to shut the place down. Then your fucking cousins walk in. I haven't seen those dudes since high school. They look good. I'm sure Brad's got some kids. What's Chad doin'?"

"Ha! You're right. Chad's on the coast somewhere, puttin' out boat fires and saving peoples' lives and shit."

"Oh, *what up Chad.* What's he drink?"

"Sober as a gofer, homie."

"Dammit. *Of course*, he is."

I laugh.

"I can work with that," she says, "but now I've gotta put in some effort and get to know him without the social lubrication. Now it's a whole thing, Mic. Now I've gotta marry the guy! *Jesus!* It's a funeral, *Mic*. This is not the time for matchmaking. *Get it together!*"

I laugh and feel a hand on my shoulder. It's a bearded Murphy in a grey suit. We lock eyes–his eyes full of tears. He's good. We embrace. He squeezes me like it's a real funeral.

"Great to see you, my friend," he says.

This is the first moment I have to actually look around at the bar. It looks exactly the same as it always has. I assumed it'd feel different, but no. It feels just like a bar.

"Hey…you wanna see a body?" asks Murphy.

"Jesus. I thought you'd never ask."

He walks me out to the patio. As I've described before, the Shoes patio sits within the walls of the building—like a courtyard you'd see in a Frank Lloyd Wright house, but way, way trashier. It's just pea gravel, picnic tables, and a horseshoe pit. The pit runs straight down the middle of the patio and points at the opening in the building. Currently, that opening frames the view of a soon-to-be cornfield a.k.a. an old bean field that's been covered in snow for the past five months.

Normally, at the top of the patio, furthest from the cornfield, there's a little stage. Local cover bands and dad bands play here every Friday and Saturday night. Occasionally, people have tried to hold Sunday morning "cowboy church" here, but instead of gospel and country tunes, the Sunday lunch jams always take on an "I changed the words to this Mellencamp song and now it's about Jesus" tone. When I lived in town, the buddies and I would end up at this Sunday service if we stayed out too late on a Saturday night. Nothing more sobering than seeing a man wear a bowling shirt, jean shorts, and a cowboy hat live out his musical dreams. It's beautiful stuff.

But today, there's no drum set or overly large bass rig onstage. There's no portable PA system and weird little light mixer. There's no music stand holding a binder full of guitar tabs for every song you could ever hope to hear on Mix 96.7.

Today, there are some flowers, a couple of potted ferns, a coffin, and an easel holding a framed photo of Arthur Fischer—or something that looks like Arthur Fischer.

"Jesus Christ!" I exclaim. "It's so..."

"I know," says Murphy. "I burst into tears when I first saw the photo."

"Yeah...where'd you guys get that picture? Why is his hair so long? Why does it make me feel so strange?"

The photo was in a 2ft x 4ft gold frame and the quality of something between a Christmas card and a high school senior photo. It's an up-close portrait of what appears to be an 18-year-old Fischer, but with a receding hairline, wearing a green sweater and posing on a white background. The photo is very cloudy, very Photoshopped, and very upsetting to the eye. It sits in an uncanny valley, like the 2004 movie version of *Polar Express*.

"Well...we couldn't really find any nice, normal photos of Fischer, so we took this photo of him laughing at some party and tried to make it work, but he was still holding a beer, and we thought that's no good for a funeral. So, we kept zooming in—trying to crop out the beer, ya know—but then

Doobs pointed out that there was someone's naked ass in the background of the photo. So, we decided that we needed to take out the background. I got so stressed, 'cause we were getting into crunch time, but I remember this girl, Chelsea, who lives in the apartment above me, does photography stuff, so I asked her if she could Photoshop the background out of this picture of Fish. She said 'no problem.' So, she sent me the new pic and it looked so scary because it's just this obviously intoxicated photo of Fisher on this white background. I had her change the color a few times but it just kept looking crazier, so I asked her if we could Photoshop his head onto a different body. She said 'probably.' So we tried to do that, but none of the bodies we found online really looked like Fish's. Then Doobs said that he remembered this time when Fish needed to borrow a shirt and that Fish and I wear the same shirt size."

"Jesus. So..."

"Yeah...so we had Chelsea from upstairs take photos of me and then she doctored Fish's face onto my body."

"Wow. And you didn't want to Photoshop his whole head onto your body? Just *his* face onto *your* head and body?"

"I think she did a great job. It looks just like him. I think she's got a real future ahead of her."

"That is *somethin'*."

"I know. And sure, we could've just called his mom and tried to find a better photo, but I'm not a fuckin' coward. This isn't the season for cowards. This is a season for bravery."

"I have no words."

Just then, I feel a warm hand on my shoulder and turn around to see a man in a giant, five-button, black pinstripe suit with giant lapels.

“Thank you for coming,” he says. “So glad you could make it. I’m so sorry for your loss.”

It was Daniel “Double Dip” DuBois.

“Doobs!” I exclaim as we embrace. “I probably haven’t hugged you since Covid hit.”

“My friend, it’s been too long. You look well.”

“You too, Doobs! Look at your suit. How many buttons does that jacket have?”

“Enough. And look at this!” He turns around to reveal the back of the jacket. “It’s got tails.”

“Amazing.”

“He spent days trying to find the right suit,” says Murph. “It’s very difficult to find a giant pinstripe suit with tails these days.”

“I can only imagine,” I say.

Doobs opens the jacket to reveal a paisley liner.

“Christ!” I exclaim. “Pinstripes and paisley?”

“That sounds like the name of a store that just sells costume jewelry and scarves to suburban mothers,” laughs Murphy.

“I kept all the tags, too,” says Doobs. “I’m going to try and return it on Monday, So don’t let me puke on myself. OK, Mic?”

I laugh. “Deal.”

“These aren’t the days for puking on ourselves, Mic. These are the days for bravery,” repeats Murphy.

“What the fuck does that even mean?” asks Doobs angrily.

“Relax, Doobs. You gotta keep your stress down,” says Murph. “We’ve got the whole weekend ahead of us.”

“He’s right, Doobs. And hey! Nice decorations, bud!” I exclaim, gesturing towards the glitter-covered cardboard bubble lettering above the stage.

SORRY 4 YOUR LOSS

“Classy stuff, Doobs.”

“You’re tellin’ me! The fuckin assholes at Party Palace were out of letter F’s, so I couldn’t even spell ‘FISCHER.’ And now his Funfetti funeral sign looks like the title of a fucking Prince song.”

“I think it’s perfect, bud.”

“Yeah, it’s way better with the number ‘4’ rather than the word ‘FOR.’ Fish would’ve liked it this way,” says Murphy.

"Speaking of…did he ever come up with a plan for how's he's going to tell Dave that he's not dead?"

"He's gotta have something in mind, but when I talked to him this morning, he was just planning on going to the breadstick place in the mall and carb-loading for his own funeral," I say.

"Jesus," says Doobs. "This is going to be a disaster. All my work for nothing."

I laugh. "Relax! He'll come up with something. He always does. It's his funeral. We should give him the benefit of the doubt."

Just then, we hear what sounds like a muffled group of people yelling, and the front door of Shoes swings open. In walks, in almost slow motion, Ginger (The Crawfish King of Columbus), Johnny Waterbottle, and Michael Popper.

Now, traditionally, when these three individuals get together, things are known to get messy. The three of them have always taken on a *Three Amigos* sort of mentality. They were inseparable as kids, and all the way through college. It's an unhealthy relationship to anyone who only knows them tangentially, but they're family—in the most Midwestern sense. They're ride-or-die homies. And they have clearly been pre-gaming since early this morning.

"Oh, my!" says Murphy. "It's the brunch boys!"

All three of them laugh. In high school, one Friday a month, these fools would skip class, go to brunch, and get absolutely lampshades-on-their-heads drunk. Sometimes at a restaurant. Sometimes at someone's parents' house.

Sometimes they'd bring a picnic to the park. They loved nothing more than getting dressed up and getting sauced, and today was no exception. They roll into Shoes with matching sear sucker suits that are far too small for them.

"Guys! This is messed up," says Ginger. "I've never been so excited."

Johnny laughs. "We just left Café Ronda." (Café Ronda is what they called Ginger's mom's house on brunch day.)

"She made us carb load via pancakes and now I got the sugar shakes," says Ging.

"Always great seeing Ronda," says Pop, "and I think she finally sees me for the man I am becoming."

"You have to stop talking about my mom, dude. It's funny, like, one time," says Ging.

"I know! And these dudes haven't heard it yet, so this is my one time," says Pop. "But seriously. Ronda has my number. She knows how to find me. It's all about timing, you know."

"You need to spend less time thinking about my mom and more time thinking about what the hell you're going to say to Kelsey when she shows up."

Ginger and Pop go back and forth like this for three minutes or so. The rest of us sidebar.

…

"They been doing this all morning?" asks Murph.

“Yeah—since Pop started buttering up to Ronda at breakfast,” says Johnny.

“They’re both pretty sloppy already,” says Doobs. “I like your suits. Are those the same ones from High School?”

“Yeah, dude. My mom found mine in a closet a few months ago. I sent the boys a pic of it. They both still had theirs, so I was like ‘Dude…we should wear them to the funeral!’ And they were like, ‘Dude…*yeah!’* I thought we were joking, but I showed up to Café Ronda and they both had theirs on, so they made me go home and put mine on before we rolled over here.”

“Damn. They’re so small,” I say.

“Yeah. I think I’m 50lbs heavier than I was in high school. I could barely button the pants. I’m glad I bought the suit so big, and seersucker has some nice stretch to it. Very underrated fabric.”

“You got any idea of what Kels knows or doesn’t know?” asks Murphy.

“Not really. Pop keeps blowing off my questions about it. He’ll change the subject or go off about something else. I’ve got a bad feeling about it. Not a *really* bad feeling, just that ‘Oh crap’ sorta feeling. Like…Kels was a monster at pulling some shit back in the day, so if the two of them are conspiring again, at Dave’s expense no less, then I’ve just got a bad feeling about it.”

“Yeah, and all bets are off if Pop’s already this far gone,” says Doobs.

“Oh! They’re not drunk,” Johnny says.

“What do you mean?” I ask.

“Well…I walked into the kitchen at Ronda’s when she was mixing up her special *brunch-boy-mimosas*. It’s just orange juice, sparkling grape juice, and a little apple cider vinegar.”

“What?!” exclaims Doobs.

“I know. I asked her what the secret was. And she said she’s been making ‘em that way for us since we were kids. Which makes sense. I just always assumed Ronda was one of those ‘Well…if they’re going to get shitty, I’d rather them do it here’ sorta parents and that I had a higher alcohol tolerance since Ging and Pop were always acting really skunked after brunch. But turns out, we were gettin' served sparkling orange juice the whole time.”

“Do *they* know there’s no booze?” asks Murph.

Johnny laughs. “No way! Look at ‘em. I think it’s great. They’re fumbling over their words, left and right, just ‘cause. It’s like we’re kids again.”

“Placebo drunk!” I say.

“Amazing!” says Murph.

“So stupid,” says Doobs.

…

"Watch it, dude!" says Ginger. "I've hurt people for saying less! Just because you're a buddy doesn't mean you can talk about Ronda like..."

"For saying what? For saying what?" says Popper, raising his voice above Ginger's.

"Will you morons shut up?!" says Doobs. "We need to focus."

"Doobs is right," says Murphy, "and I wouldn't say that if it wasn't true."

"Sorry," says Pop. "This place looks awesome, guys. Great sign, Doobs."

"Yeah!" says Ginger. "What the fuck is going on with this picture of Fish?"

"It's Fish's face on my head and body," says Murphy.

"But we don't have time to explain it again," says Doobs. "Ms. Fish is gonna be here any minute. Then other people are going to start showing up. Then *Dave's* going to show up, so we need to get our shit together."

"Oh, dudes...Connie's in the parking lot with all the other Fishes right now," says Johnny.

"Yeah. She was here when we pulled up," says Ging. "She's just out there cuttin' up with people."

"What do you mean? Like Fish's whole family's just standing out there in the parking lot?" asks Murph.

“Yeah…but like there’s maybe fifty people out there,” says Pop.

“Woof,” says Doobs. “I’m stressed.”

“We haven’t seen anybody but Meghan and you guys,” says Murph.

“Well, shit…There’s a damn hootenanny goin’ on in the parking lot,” says Ginger.

And sure enough, as if they’d manifested it, we see a mob of at least fifty people come around the side of the building into the courtyard. In the front of the pack, talking with her entire body, is Connie Fischer, mother of our late(ish) friend Arthur.

Connie Fischer is the person you want cutting your hair in town. Connie is everything you want her to be and more. She’s boisterous. She’s loud. She’s quick on her feet. She can talk for hours and hours and hours and hours about nothing or everything, all at once. She can go deep. She can stay shallow. She’s the cheapest therapist in town and the most expensive haircut ($75 for a cut and root touch-up), but she’s worth every penny.

Today, she’s wearing a black dress and a little black veil. She’s crying, but only because she’s laughing so hard. She keeps dabbing her eyes so as to not upset her eyeliner. As she gets closer to us, she realizes who she’s looking at and exclaims,

“Oh my gosh! Look at you guys! You’re full-grown men! I just can’t handle this. I got so emotional on the way here. Then I got myself together and all these people were hanging around, and I thought, 'Oh my gosh. What are all these people doin' here?' Then I started to recognize some folks and they were like, 'Oh, we're just so excited about the funeral! We read about it in the paper and thought it was hilarious. Your son's friends must be crazy. But we just think it's so fun.' And then I was like, 'Oh my gosh…they're all here for Arthur!' I was so touched. It's like they're here for his actual funeral. But he's not actually dead, so that makes it way more fun. And it's just a great excuse to see everybody! I'm so glad you boys are here! I miss you guys!"

"We miss you too, Ms. Fish! How you holdin' up?" asks Ginger.

"You stop it, Ginger! You guys are going to make me cry again! And why are you guys's suits so small?" she says, gesturing towards Johnny, Pop, and Ginger.

Just then, she seems to part the six of us and sees the stage. Coffin, flowers, ferns, and the haunting portrait.

We are silent. She is silent. We're looking at her for a cue on how to react. She doesn't react. We are, as a group, overwhelmed by a mother, looking at her son's casket. I begin to get emotional, as does the rest of the group. We're looking around at each other, unsure of what to do. Connie walks up to the casket and puts her hand on it. The humidity in the room rises. Then she looks over at the photo on the stand.

She begins to cry. No one says a word. The bar is silent.

She composes herself and turns to address us. She looks each one of us in the eyes in silence. She begins to tear up. Then the dam breaks into tears. She hangs her head, shaking in silence. Unable to take a breath. Pop and I help her down off the stage. She stands there looking around at us, tears and mascara rolling down her face, shaking her head. Then she looks down, pauses, lets out a little whimper, wipes her eyes, and looks up at Murphy.

"Is that your body in that photo?" She asks him.

We are silent.

"Yes, ma'am."

The bar is silent.

"God..." she says, pausing. "You guys are fucking crazy."

She grabs Murphy's face and gives him a huge, comical kiss on the lips. She pulls his face away and yells,

"Bar's open! Long live Fishy Fisherson!"

At this point, the bar goes absolutely wild.

People are walking around, toasting with full pitchers of beer.

People are standing on tables singing "Auld Lang Syne."

Murph makes a signal to Doobs. Doobs nods and releases a net of black balloons on the unsuspecting bar.

At this point, the 100+ people packed into this bar are losing their damn minds. Meghan rings the bell to signal that a train's coming. Just beautiful timing.

And like something out of a movie, a chorus of strangers is dancing to a drunken rendition of “Oh Susannah” as black balloons rain down from the sky.

A train flies by in the background of a would-be dim-lit bar, in the middle of the day.

Six friends stand in front of a coffin, looking at a hundred people that are having the best time for the stupidest reason.

Murphy makes eye contact with me from across this group of friends and points at the front door. We all turn our heads to see, through the dramatically slow movement of the falling black balloons, two people that have obviously just walked into this chaos, Dave and Kelsey.

—

Dave is dressed in a well-tailored dark grey suit. His hair—long, but in place—movie star hair. He’s wearing sunglasses and has obviously been through a roller coaster of emotions on the way here.

The Kelsey we grew up with was a tough yet objectively good-looking tomboyish character. Girl-next-door-level cute. She’s the nerdy/artsy character in the 90s rom-com. She’s Velma in Scooby-Doo. Then at some point, someone takes her glasses off, lets her hair down, and the whole school’s like, “Wow...who is she?” But instead of her realizing her potential and ending up with the jock, who was wrong about her the whole time, she steals the jock’s car and drives off into the sunset by herself with a middle finger out the window.

Kelsey, today, is *that* person, a decade and a half later. She's very aware of her potential and very successful at doing what she does. She's able to take on whatever situation is thrown her way. Under normal circumstances, her funeral garb would consist of appropriate but flattering attire, but today she's got on a little black dress—the kind of dress you reserve for going out on the town to get laid, not the kind you'd wear to a funeral.

"Jesus," says Doobs. "This weekend's gonna be rough."

As Dave and Kelsey walk towards us, a wave seems to creep across the entire bar—as people are either looking at *that* girl in *that* dress or realizing that *this* dude with *that* girl is *the* dude that doesn't realize that his friend isn't really dead.

I look at Pop and realize that all the other guys are making eyes at him as well. He drifts to the back of the group, cowering in his overly small seersucker suit, Meghan happens to be standing right behind us with a tray of black Jell-O shots in Dixie cups. He looks at the tray, then back up at her.

"Please," she says, gesturing towards the shots with her eyes.

Pop takes two of the little cups and slams them one after the other, the second cup awkwardly dropping remnants of black jello onto his weird little suit jacket. He puts the cups back on the tray.

"Relax," says Meghan, pushing him back towards the group. "You'll be all right."

Pop turns his attention back to Dave and Kelsey. Dave, looking right at Connie, Fischer's mom, with tears in his eyes. Connie starts tearing up again. She moves toward Dave and gives him a big hug.

At this point, all of us are really feeling the gravity of the situation. This interaction between Connie and Dave will set the tone for the rest of the day. We didn't even get the opportunity to talk to Connie about what Dave knows and doesn't know, or what Kelsey knows or *may* know.

"I'm so sorry, Ms. Fish," Dave says.

Connie lets out a little yelp, somewhere between a loud sneeze and a laugh. She recomposes herself while holding onto Dave. "Me too…I'm so sorry, too."

We all look at each other and back at them, afraid that she's going to blow this thing wide open.

"So sorry about your bachelor party," she says, squeezing him tighter. "I know Arty was really looking forward to it."

We look around once again and then back at her. She winks at us.

That wink is Connie's blessing. She laid the sauce on thick for us. She even called Fish "Arty." Only Connie can call him Arty. It's her baby name for him. She was giving us permission to mess Dave up, regardless of how morally questionable it is.

Connie pulls away from Dave, giving him a good long look in the eyes. Then she turns her attention to Kelsey.

"Ms. Kelsey...*wow*! You look gorgeous!" she says. "You're so grown up. Look how grown up you guys are." She gives Kels a big hug.

"Great to see you, Ms. Fish. So sorry about Schwimmer." (Fischer, Fish, Swimmer, Schwimmer.)

"Oh, me too, dear." At this point, Connie grabs Kelsey by the hands, looking deep into her eyes. She's studying Kelsey's face, trying to figure out what she knows and doesn't know. Kelsey lets out the tiniest smirk. Connie pulls her back in for another hug. "Me too. I'm so sorry, too."

Connie pulls away once again, smiling and eventually letting go of her. "I just can't get over how much you guys have grown. Kelsey, I probably haven't seen you in fifteen years."

Mothers always speak in terms of how much people have "grown." They're really just commenting on how much older we are, compared to the last time they've seen us. For the most part, "growth" is a positive. You only have to worry when they start saying that you've "filled out."[22]

---

[22] If you're a man, "you've really filled out" means that you used to be a skinny little twerp and now you look like an adult, or if you weren't a skinny little twerp, it just means that you look fat.

If you're a woman, "you've really filled out" means that you got your boobs. Connie would never tell Kelsey that she's "really filled out." She's more civil than that, so "growth" will have to do.

Dave approaches each one of us, heading towards Doobs first. Dave goes in for a hug, but Doobs cuts him off with a handshake.

“So glad you could make it,” he says with a straight face while wearing a paisley-lined, pinstripe suit with tails.

“Wouldn’t miss it,” says Dave.

Dave moves down the line, like he’s at a sub shop, hugging each of us and saying our names in a somber tone.

“Mic. Great to see you, bud.”

“Hey, Dave.”

“Murph. Great to see you, man.”

“You too, Dave.”

“Ginger. Nice suit.”

“Thanks, Dave.”

“Johnny. Nice suit.”

“Thanks, Dave.”

“Mr. Popper. Nice suit.”

“Thanks, Dave.”

“Hey! You guys all have the same suit on.”

"Yeah, Dave," says Pop, acknowledging Dave's slowness while also realizing that Dave looks *way* more put together than himself or any of our other friends.

"Man…it's just great to see you guys," says Dave, genuinely.

"You too, Dave," says Ginger. "Sorry it couldn't be under better circumstances."

"Me…" Dave gets choked up, then recomposes himself. "Me too, Ging. Me too."

There's a bit of an awkward silence at this point. If our friend was really dead, we'd all be trying to fill this awkward space with small talk and genuineness. But fortunately, he's not dead, so everyone stands here in their completely ridiculous funeral attire, reflecting on the nature of our own sick creation. The group then turns their attention to Kelsey.

"Hey, guys. Great to see you," she says.

"You too, Kels," says Johnny.

She looks right at Popper. He looks back at her. Then both of them dodge each other's eyes. We all notice, except for Dave. Dave's attention has been captured by the casket that's sitting behind us.

We all shift our attention to see how Dave's going to react to the coffin and the outrageously Photoshopped portrait of Fish's face on Murphy's body.

Dave puts his hand on the casket. Similar to earlier, the whole bar seems to understand what's happening, and the place goes silent. Then Dave kneels at the casket. The crowd and all of us start to murmur and look around nervously. Dave, while kneeling, attempts to make the sign of the cross. (Dave is very much *not* Catholic. This is something he's seen in movies and feels like he's supposed to do.) He stands and kisses the casket. (Also something he's seen in movies.) Then he finally looks at the large and very fucked-up photo beside the casket. He pauses.

Then, from somewhere behind us, a familiar voice pierces the silence.

"Jesus Christ."

The bar instantly bounces back to normal, leaving Dave kneeling at the casket, unfazed by the change in tone.

The rest of us turn to see the breakers of the silence, Tyler and Travis Thompson.

"Godammit," Mumbles Doobs to himself. "The fucking Thompson Twins."

"*Shout. Shout. Let it all out…"* sings Johnny, quietly.

I laugh. "That's Tears for Fears, dude."

He laughs. "Oh shit! That's right. The fuckin Thompson Twins, though. Gets me every time."

As they approach us, Kelsey and Popper make eyes at each other, again. Everybody notices, except for Dave, again.

"I don't like Pop and Kelsey looking at each other," says Murphy. "It makes me nervous."

"You and me both," says Ginger, "but I don't hate it as much as the Thompson brothers."

"What's happenin', ya big freaks?" says Travis.

"Yeah, what's happenin', fools?" says Tyler.

The Thompson twins are wearing matching black, wide lapel, power suits with big, fat neckties. Similar to Doobs's getup, but without the tails. This is an outfit you'd likely see on someone from the 1999 NBA draft, or maybe a pre-prison sentence Donald Trump, Jr.

"Hey, guys," I say. "Glad you could make it."

"Wouldn't miss it. We love the Fish man," says Tyler.

"We *loved* the Fish man," Travis corrects. "Past tense, because he's no longer with us."

"Oh, right, right!" says Tyler. "So sorry for your loss. Our loss. His loss…of life. So sorry."

"Jesus," says Murphy softly, retreating and leaving me here to fend for myself with these monsters.

"Yeah…we're sorry too," I say. "Thanks for the hookup at the monument. I think it's going to push this thing over the top."

"Happy to help," says Tyler.

I give the Thompsons a quick shoulder pat as if to say, "Good seeing you but I'm in the middle of something," and attempt to survey the room.

The entire bar is slammed with people. Connie is holding court in the corner of the room. People continue to walk past the casket and scoff at the strange photo, as it is very alarming.

Meghan and her mother, Tracy (who has seemed to appear out of the blue), are serving beers as fast as they can. This amount of people all at once would send me into a panic if I were behind the bar, but Meghan and Tracy are trained professionals. Tracy catches my glance and blows me a kiss. She's as calm and collected as ever. Rock star shit.

The gang is keeping to themselves but within the crowd. Doobs is walking through the mob towards the rest of the crew, holding eight beers above his head.[23] Pop and Kelsey are talking and laughing—a good sign, but dangerous for all sorts of reasons.

I see some people that I recognize from my childhood: neighborhood people, Fish's extended family, my extended family. It's exactly who'd be at a funeral, plus some. But instead of the awkward small talk and wiping of tearful eyes, everybody's drinking and having a great time.

Then, out of the crowd, I spot a man with a strange, pointy beard wearing sunglasses and a plaid newsy hat, like you'd see someone's retired father wear to an Irish pub or an open-mic night at a coffee shop.

We make eye contact (though I can't be sure because he's wearing sunglasses). Regardless, he notices that I see him and starts to head towards the door. I start to approach him. He keeps turning around to see if I'm following him, which

---

[23] An impressive and very Midwestern skill, if there ever was one.

I certainly am at this point. Then all of the sudden, I feel something cold down my back. I turn around to see a person that I recognize from a lifetime ago.

“I iced you,” he says. “Bros icing bros.”[24]

“That’s not what that is,” I say, pulling the ice cube from the bottom of my shirt.[25]

“Wait…I know you,” he says. “You used to work at a bar up at Put-in-Bay.”

“Yup,” I say, regretfully. “That’s right.”

“You don’t remember me, do you?” he says.

“Of course, I remember you,” I say.

“Oh yeah? Well…what’s my name?” he asks.

---

[24] “Bros icing bros” was a phenomenon that occurred between 2000 and 2010, where college-aged males would hide a Smirnoff Ice (a bottled malt beverage with an alcohol content similar to beer and a flavor profile similar to spoiled hard candy) in hopes that one of their “bros” would come across said Smirnoff Ice. Upon the surprise discovery of this beverage, the discoverer was to get down on one knee and chug the disgusting libation. Common hiding places to come across one of these bottles include, but are not limited to: pizza boxes, back packs, other boxes of more socially acceptable beverages, underneath a couch cushion, etc.

[25] Our friend seems to have heard the phrase “bros icing bros” and taken it upon himself to decide that it’s probably just dudes putting ice cubes down the backs of each other’s shirts. It’s innocent enough, but completely inappropriate at a funeral, obviously.

Meghan rushes up to us.

"Get the fuck out of here, Donnie," she says.[26]

"Excuuuuse me, Meg!" says Donnie.

"Excuse yourself, dude," she replies.

"What the hell are you doing here, Donnie?" asks Tracy, who has made her way over to us.

Now, I know how Meg knows Donnie. She worked on the island, same as me. But how does Tracy know him? Is he *that* infamous? I've never seen him this far inland before.

"Wait…Tracy, how do you guys know each other?" I ask.

"Ha! This dreadful creature is, in fact, my younger brother," she replies.

I am shocked.

"Wait," says Meghan. "You didn't know that?"

I laugh nervously. "No, I did not."

---

[26] Donnie, as you may remember, is the regular from me and Meghan's old haunt on the island. Floor-length fur coat. Rag-top Buick. Picking up strange divorcees at the bar. Stealing ice out of the ice machine. You remember Donnie. How could you forget Donnie?

“Yeah,” she says. “That’s why this fool used to come into the bar on the island all the time. He knew that I would never permanently remove him from the bar.”

“Though you easily could have,” adds Tracy.

“Touché,” says Donnie, curtsying and tipping his imaginary hat.

“And honestly, I viewed it as a public service,” says Meghan. “The more time he spent at the my bar, the less time he spent at any other bar, irritating every other person on that Godforsaken island.”

“So dramatic, Meg,” adds Donnie as Tracy slaps him in the back of the head.

“*But*,” adds Tracy. “He’s not allowed to come in here.”

“Why?” I ask.

“Because he scares off the customers! When my dad opened this place, he only had two rules for us: No getting wrecked during business hours and *no scaring off the customers*. This fool is a walking violation of both rules.”

“That’s so harsh, sis. But I’m afraid she is accurate,” Donnie says, turning to me. “I have made a life of scaring customers from various establishments and that is why I’m happy to announce that I am now making a *career* of it.”

“I will regret asking this, but what does that mean?” asks Tracy, begrudgingly.

“Well, my darling, you are now looking at the CEO and President of Donnie’s Dark Desires, LLC.”

“Is that like a weird sex shop or something?” asks Meghan.

“No. Why would you think it’s a sex shop?”

“Because ‘Donnie’s Dark Desires’ sounds like a sex shop,” I interject.

“It’s not a sex shop, guys!” he exclaims.

“Well, what is it?” asks Tracy.

“It’s my new haunted house business,” he says.

“You bought the haunted house behind the old jail?” Tracy asks.

“The one with the corn maze where that kid went missing?” Meghan asks.

“Yeah…” Donnie says.

“I thought they shut that place down,” I say.

“Well…they did.”

“But you bought it?” asks Tracy.

“Yeah.” Says Donnie.

“Why?”

“What do you mean, ‘Why?’ Because it’s a haunted house!” explains Donnie.

“I know,” says Tracy, “but why do you need a haunted house?”

“For my haunted house business,” says Donnie.

“Jesus Christ,” I say, looking at my watch.

Tracy and Donnie go back and forth on the merits and seasonal structure of a haunted house business, along with the morally sketchy nature of a haunted house with a missing children’s report hanging over its head. Meghan and I stand here and watch these two siblings trade blows for an eternity, attempting to find a spot to interrupt the bickering.

“Donnie…Donnie…Donnie…” I say, trying to get Donnie’s attention. “Donnie…*DONNIE!*”

Eventually, he turns to me. “Yeah?”

“Why are you here, Donnie?”

“Yeah, Donnie. Why are you here?” asks Meghan.

“For the funeral.”

“Yeah…but why?” I ask.

Just then, Travis and Tyler Thompson approach us. I am now entering Doobs’ personal hell.

“Donnie Baby! What’s shakin?” says Travis.

The Thompsons' speech patterns and vernacular are so outrageously confident and, for lack of a better term, *douchey*, that you'd love to hate 'em. But in this particular instance, I find them highly entertaining—I wouldn't let them babysit my kids, but it's outrageous dialogue.

"You telling these fine folks about Triple D's House of Horrors?" asks Tyler.

"Wait…how do you guys know Donnie?" I ask.

"We just helped our man Dirty D close the deal on his new haunted house endeavor. It's the best haunted house in town. This fall…you guys…you've gotta go!" says Travis.

"Well, it's the *only* haunted house in town," I say.

"We know!" says Travis. "That's why it's *the best*."

"You know it," says Tyler. "You know what they say, 'There's no competition like no competition.'"

"Nobody says that," says Tracy.

"Sure, they do! Here's my card," says Tyler, handing Tracy his business card.

TYLER THOMPSON

JUNIOR EXECUTIVE

SCHUSTER, SHRINER, AND SONS

"There's No Competition like No Competition"

“Jesus.” Says Tracy.

Meghan and I lean over to look at the card.

“Man…that’s the worst thing I’ve ever seen,” says Meghan.

“Yeah…” I say. “Is that font at the bottom…”

“Yeah…Papyrus,” says Travis. “They’re a little cheeky. I know. Designed them myself. I went through a big design phase a few years ago. You gotta diversify, right, my guys? Everyone in the city’s been real big on minimalism. But that shit is boring. It’s just like colors and squiggles and stuff with boring-ass font. But if that’s what they want, that’s what you got to give ‘em. So, boom! Now we got a graphics design company.”

“Give him your card,” says Tyler.

“Oh word!” says Travis, cruising through all the interior pockets of his jacket.

He pulls out a bright pink business card.

Travis Thompson

CEO and Lead Designer

Designs by Travis

"There's No Design like No Design"

“Wow,” I say. “That is somethin’.”

“Sure is!” says Travis.

“That’s great, guys. But we’re actually in the middle of some family business right now,” says Tracy, gesturing to Donnie.

“Oh shit!” says Tyler. “You guys are all family? That’s crazy!”

“Donnie! You’re gonna have to give ‘em the family discount!” says Travis.

“Ha!” laughs Meghan. “Yeah…when you get your sketchy-ass haunted house up and rolling, I fully expect the family discount.”

“Oh, definitely!” says Travis. “But I meant for today. Those miles are going to add up. Yo, Mic! How you not going to tell me you and Donnie is kin? That’s crucial information.”

At this point, I am very confused. I haven’t thought about Donnie in years. And why would I even consider telling the Thompson twins (who I haven’t seen in fifteen years) that I know *Donnie?* How am I supposed to know that *they* even know that *Donnie* exists? And *why the hell is Donnie here*? This situation is fragile enough as-is, but now I’m listening to a perverted, floor-length-fur-coat-wearing ghost from my past talk to the fucking *Thompson twins* about some haunted house. These are all concerns that I’d like to voice, but instead, I pause and go with,

“What? Donnie and I are not related. Donnie and Ms. Tracy, here, are siblings. Meghan is Tracy’s daughter—which means she’s Donnie’s…niece?”

“Yes,” says Meghan. “You got it. Keep goin’.”

“But…what do you mean when you say ‘for today?’ You said something about giving us the ‘family discount *for today*.’ What does *‘for today’* mean?”

They look at me, confused. There’s an awkward silence. Then Travis starts to speak.

“Well, Mic…if you and Donnie aren’t family, you can’t expect him to give you the family discount.”

“I don’t care! *What are you talking about? Why is Donnie here? What is going on?”* I demand, calmly.

“Oh,” says Tyler, “Donnie’s the man with the hearse.”

“What?”

“Yeah…I figured that you guys didn’t remember to rent a hearse and when we went to close on the haunted house, the dude who used to own it handed Donnie a pair of keys to the hearse that he used to use for advertising. So, I was like, ‘Boom, Donnie! I got your first client right here!’ And I told him about the funeral and all this shit. Figured even if you guys *did* have a hearse, there’s nothin’ like showing up to a *fake funeral* with a *real-ass hearse*, right? Like, it’s *killer* advertising,” says Tyler.

“*Killer advertising*,” confirms Travis.

I’m speechless at this point and turn to Meghan.

"First off," she says, "I don't think you should say '*killer* advertising' in regards to a haunted house that still has a missing children's report attached to it."

Travis and Tyler look at each other and nod. "That's fair," they say in unison.

"Second," Meghan continues, "I'm sure Mic and these fools got a hearse, already."

They all turn to me. I am expressionless.

"Dammit, Mic," she says.

At this point, Doobs and Murph are walking past, and I notice them in my peripheral.

"Hey, Doobs," I say. He turns to me and then away quickly, realizing that the Thompsons have me cornered. Doobs can't handle the Thompsons, but I wrangle him into the conversation anyway.

"Hey, Doobs. We already have a hearse, right?"

"What? Why would we need a hearse for a fake funeral?"

"Doobie baby!" says Travis. "Long time, amigo! You look well. I like that suit. Look at the tails! Look at the stripes. Tasteful, bro."

"Don't try to gas me up, Thompson. This is a fragile situation. Don't fuck with me."

"Geeez…" says Tyler. "Watch that blood presh, Daddy."

"Doobster…listen. Don't worry about the hearse. We gotchu, baby," says Travis.

"We don't need a hearse," says Murph, realizing that someone needs to step between Doobs and the Thompsons. This conversation has obviously made me weak. I can only fight so much.

"This is going to be a New Orleans-style funeral procession," says Murph. "We're carrying the casket. We don't need a hearse."

"Well, how the hell are y'all getting the casket up to the lake?" asks Tyler.

"Shit…I don't know, we're going to put it in the back of Josh-Josh's truck or something."

All of the sudden, the hair on the back of my neck stands up, as I hear a voice behind me.

"Where the hell *is* Josh-Josh?" says Dave.

Fearful that he'd heard too much, I try to cover. "Dave! You remember the Thompsons…"

"Holy shit," says Dave. *"The fucking Thompson twins!"*

"Dave!" exclaims Travis.

"Look at you beauties!" exclaims Dave. "What are you guys doing here? Mic! It's the *fucking Thompson Twins!"*

"Yeah, Dave. I know!"

Dave loves the Thompson twins. When the Thompsons were in high school, Dave was going through a townie phase after failing out of college. He often found himself buying beer for the then underaged Thompsons and tagging along with them on their wild escapades. In those days, at a party, I'd typically throw in the towel somewhere between midnight and 1:30 am, but I've heard stories of Dave and the Thompsons raging past sunrise, building stilts out of beer cans, and testing their mortality.

They gassed each other up. Three yes-men with nothing to lose. They were the antithesis of the rhetorical parent asking, "Well…if they were going to jump off a bridge, would you do that too?"

"I dunno…probably," they'd say. "We jumped off it last week and it was great!"

This is an element that I didn't consider when involving the Thompsons this weekend.

"What the hell are you guys doing here?" Dave asks again.

"Well, obviously, my friend, we're here to pay respects to Big Fish," says Tyler.

"One of the great ones," says Travis. "Gone too soon."

"Couldn't have said it better, myself," agrees Dave.

Tyler continues, overselling the comical nature of their dialogue like a bad stage actor or a child in a horror movie, while Travis stares straight at me, maniacally, brow furrowed like he's doing a Jack Nicholson impression. "And congratulations to you, my friend. I was thrilled to hear of your engagement. Kelsey is one lucky lady."

Then Travis picks up where Tyler left off while Tyler turns and stares straight at me–as if they had choreographed it. "Or maybe *you're* the lucky one. The Kelsey we knew in grade school has certainly blossomed into a beautiful woman."

"Thanks, guys! We're very excited," says Dave, not seeming to notice the strangeness of their tone.

Tyler starts speaking. Again, Travis staring straight at Murphy this time. "So sorry to hear that you had to cancel your bachelor party. It sounds like the boys had quite the ordeal planned."

They switch off again, Travis speaking and Tyler staring straight at Murph. "But certainly, even more sorry to hear of the passing of our good man, Artemus Fischerson. What a tragedy. What a loss."

"Yes…it's been a very hard week," says Dave, still not noticing how thick they're laying it on.

Now both Travis and Tyler look straight at Dave.

Tyler starts speaking, "I'm so glad we're able to help in any way we can. The funeral home reached out to us, knowing that we were friends of Fischers and also operating partners in a small fleet of formal vehicle rentals."

Travis continues, "… and though we mostly function in the nightlife, black car, limousine business, we just happened to acquire a hearse and I think I speak for both me and my brother when I say that we're honored to be of service in these trying times."

Both Tyler and Travis then simultaneously turn to Doobs, daring him to say otherwise, Doobs's blood boiling.

I try to cut the tension, rubbing Doobs's shoulders like I'm trying to get a dog to calm down. By this point, most of the gang has started listening in.

"Yes. Tyler and Travis have been a great help this week," I say.

"That's great," says Dave. "But, where is Josh-Josh?"

I look at the rest of the gang. And they all seem to be looking around at each other as well.

Then Kelsey, who's been quiet up until now, softly exclaims, "No way!"

We all turn around and look to see what she sees.

It's what appears to be a giant squid floating by the bar. I look at my watch. 12:08. I look up at the gang.

"Shit," says Ginger. "It has begun."

Everyone seems to slowly scramble out of the bar and into the parking lot.

By the time I fight through the crowd to see what sort of situation we're dealing with, I understand that we are in way over our heads.

Out on the street, I see a line of twenty vehicles surrounded by a couple hundred people. In the front, my cousins hanging out the window of a fire truck. Behind them, a few pickup trucks pulling various trailers decorated like sea creatures and sporting vinyl signs for the PTO, the local grocery, and the farmers' co-op. Behind that, a big old dually pulling a very elaborate squid on what appears to be a triple-axle car trailer. Behind them, the high school marching band, some 150 kids, currently in formation, the drumline keeping time.

Behind the marching band, in front of a group of mimes on ATVs, and right in front of the bar, I see what is very possibly one of the coolest things I've ever seen: an extra-large tow truck completely covered in flowers, the only visible part of the truck being the windshield. The juxtaposition of such a big vehicle completely covered in flowers is truly awesome. The grill is covered in flowers. The lights are covered in flowers. There's a skirt over the wheels, also covered in flowers. The truck isn't painted, it's *covered in real flowers*. On the side of the truck, spelled out in sunflowers, "Long Live Arthur Fischer!" The door to the truck opens, revealing our good man, Joshua Joshua. I burst into tears of joy. A true hero emerges from the chaos.

He jogs up to us.

"We gotta go guys. We're on a schedule," he says.

"Great to see you, Josh-Josh," I say, embracing him.

"You too, dude. But seriously, get the casket and let's go," he says. "Y'all are right behind my truck."

"Are we walking with the casket?" I ask.

"Uh...yeah. You said this was a cool funeral procession. It's a fuckin parade, for Chrissake. Get the boys and get it together."

I turn to see Doobs, Murph, and the rest of the gang standing just outside the door of the bar. I nod to them.

Doobs and Murphy look at each other and nod back.

I fight the beer-soaked crowd to get back to the bar. I slip and fall on what I can only describe as post-winter sludge.[27]

As I stand, I see the crowd has parted to reveal Connie Fischer, her face covered in a chic black vail and smiling ear to ear. On her arm, our friend Kelsey, doing her best to keep from making eye contact with anyone. Behind them, Popper, Ginger, Johnny Waterfall, Doobs, Murphy, and Dave, all in tears, carrying the casket of their beloved friend, Arthur Fischer. Murphy and Doobs separate to allow my shoulder under the casket. The weight of the casket is real, despite there being no body inside of it. This weight seems to change the dynamic of the group. It feels as if we're really carrying our friend. We line up behind Josh-Josh's flower-covered truck, and the crowd from the bar begins to follow us. Josh-Josh comes up to us and gives an inquisitive thumbs-up.

I give him a thumbs-up back.

He reaches to his belt, pulls out a walk-in-talkie and says, "We're all clear back here."

---

[27] A patch of what was snow, turned slush, turned ice, and now covered in the tears and regrets of entire generations of people.

"Roger that, king," I hear my cousin, Chad, say back at him.

Josh-Josh hops back in his flower-covered truck and starts it up.

We begin walking, the entire crowd of the bar walking with us. Some 200 people. Other than the slow idling of engines and the whispers of people, there is nothing but the timing clicks of the marching band.

It really feels like a funeral processional. As we walk in silence, we wipe our tears and start to collect ourselves. All of us except for Dave.

Though we can't see him, Dave is seemingly having a come-to-Jesus moment. Between episodes of whimpering, he's mumbling to himself and occasionally to the spirit of Fish.

"I'm sorry I wasn't there," he says. "I miss you so much. This doesn't seem real. How can it be real? How are you gone?"

We all burst back into tears. It feels simultaneously too real and too cruel. The weight of our most elaborately cruel gag and the weight of the very real casket sends us into a collective mind-warp. The air is thick and it feels like we should put a stop to all of this.

Then, as we turn the corner onto Main Street, we see a mile's worth of people. Thousands of people here for this stupid underwater/Fish-themed parade/phony-funeral procession. We're collectively hit again, but this time with the weight of an entire community. A community that's been hit with decades of hardship and job loss and addiction, but also a community that's willing to come out and support something so utterly ridiculous, no questions asked. This is the community that birthed us and raised us, but also the community that we've left for something else. This dawns on us as a metaphor for the current state of our entire society.

As we try to navigate all of these emotions as a group, as we try to figure out where we fit into all of this, Dave starts talking to Fish again, and hits us with, "And your coffin smells like peanuts. Why does your coffin smell like peanuts?"

Right on cue, the drumline starts tapping and ushers in a rendition of "Under the Sea" from *The Little Mermaid.*

—

As the gang and I walk through the parade, we can't really speak to one another. We didn't really take into account what carrying a coffin for a mile and a half would look like.

It's a lot of time to think. It's a lot of time to process.

Me, Doobs, and Murphy are thinking about what the hell we've done and how we're going to get out of it. Ginger's thinking about how he got us into this parade situation in the first place. Johnny's thinking about how cool parades are. Pop's thinking about how hot Kelsey looks and wondering why the hell she'd want to be with someone as gullible as Dave.

Somewhere during the second verse of the marching band's rendition of Styx's "Come Sail Away," our friend Dave has another moment. He starts singing the words to the song.

I…look to…the sea,

Reflections in the waves spark my memory,

Some happy, some sad.

I think of childhood friends and the dreams we had.

By the time that last line shows itself, the crowd of people we're surrounded by takes note and starts singing along with him. Building all the while.

We live happily forever,

So the story goes.

But somehow we missed out,

On that pot of gold.

But we'll try the best that we can…

To caaaaarry on.

The drums come in, and by the time we get to the title of the song, the entire crowd is swaying and pulsating in the street. All of the sudden, the casket starts gaining momentum. Up and down. Side to side. And before you know it, the entire casket is being tossed in the air by a huge mass of people.

Come sail away,

Come sail away,

Come sail away with me.

—

This will go down as one of the most magical moments any of us will ever experience. This is as close as we'll get to the *Ferris Bueller* "Twist and Shout" scene.

Eventually, the scene calms down, and thank *God*, because the casket has been crowed-surfed some 20–30 yards from us. Dave, Pop, Ging, and Johnny are trying to catch up with it. The marching band has shifted gears to Bobby Darin's "Beyond the Sea." Murphy, Doobs, and I take a second and let the whole moment wash over us. I turn to Murphy,

"That thing's nailed shut, right?" I ask.

"For sure," says Murphy.

"What'd you fill it with to make it so heavy?" I ask.

"Peanut shells," says Doobs.

Murph and I pause and turn to him.

"That's a lot of peanuts, Doobs," says Murph.

"My brother and I have been drinking beers and throwing peanut shells in that casket all week," he says. "There's probably 100lbs of peanut shells in there."

"... and that's why the casket smells like peanuts," I say.

"For sure," says Doobs.

The crowd has begun to shift into a steady pace. Everybody blissed out from the joy they're experiencing.

We finally catch up to the gang, who's swinging the casket back and forth with a few strangers to a brass rendition of the Beach Boys' "Kokomo."

Dave looks at me and says, "I've never been so happy at a funeral."

"Me neither," I admit. "I don't think anyone has."

As we round the last corner of the parade, I turn around and take in the sight. It's ten blocks of people piled into the street. It's police officers dancing. It's dads with kids on their shoulders. It's middle-aged ladies in a conga line. It's those weird mimes on 4-wheelers, a gang of dudes on unicycles, and a couple 10ft beach balls just bouncing around amongst the crowd. It's a bunch of high school kids playing an out-of-tune yet recognizable version of Van Morrison's "Into the Mystic." It's beautiful.

We start to re-approach the bar. I realize that I'm not 100% certain of what the plan is beyond this. I know that we're heading straight to the ferry, but I haven't been able to talk to Josh-Josh or even the Thompsons about the plan. As the front of the parade and the marching band take a left at the bar, Josh-Josh's flower-covered tow truck takes a right into the parking lot of the Horseshoe.

Across the mass of people, Pop and Kelsey look at me, like, 'What's the plan?'

I turn to look at Doobs and Murphy, like, 'What's the plan?'

They look back at me, like, 'Yo…I thought *YOU* had the plan.'

Then I look back at Popper and Kels. They nod and take a collective breath, understanding that there is no plan.

As the crowd that we've accumulated over the course of the parade walks further into the parking lot of the bar, I notice that the only member of our party still holding onto the casket is Dave. I also see that Dave has noticed a hearse parked right by the entrance of the bar. For all he knows, this is the hearse that the Thompson twins have provided for transportation up to the lake. And he's not wrong, but the fact that *this* hearse is actually just part of a recent haunted house acquisition and not a legitimate (or probably even registered) vehicle is crucial information, so I try to catch up to him before the coffin makes it there.

I fight through the crowd to try and reach them as they're about to load the casket into the car. I want to yell, *'Stop!'* but that seems inappropriate, so I try to get Dave's attention with a lighter, "Hold up, Dave." Dave turns to look at me, but so does the other man loading the casket into the car, a shorter man with a strange beard wearing sunglasses and a plaid newsy hat, like you'd see someone's retired father wear to an Irish pub or an open-mic-night at a coffee shop—the same man who ran away from me earlier. I'm taken aback, as I do not see this coming. I approach them but somehow can't get the words together to keep them from shutting the door to the hearse.

The three of us, me, Dave, and the strange bearded man stand and look at each other.

"Yes, Mic?" says Dave.

"Yes, what?" I ask.

"You said, '*Hold up, Dave,*' and now I'm saying, 'Yes, Mic?'"

"Sorry. I forgot what I was going to say."

"It's been a rough day, Mic. You need to take care of yourself," he says, patting me on the shoulder.

"OK."

"Thanks for the help," Dave says to the strange man.

The strange man nods.

Dave walks away, leaving me and the strange bearded man standing behind a hearse staring at each other.

As I study the man's face, he does not react. He stands perfectly still. I look at him, confused. He just stands there silently until he reaches into his back pocket and pulls out a greasy, restaurant-style breadstick.

"Breadstick?" he asks, handing me the strange greasy appetizer.

Shit. It's Fischer.

"You son of a bitch."

"C'mon, man. Don't talk about my mom that way. Not today," he replies.

"You're playing with fire, my dude. I thought you were going to keep a low profile until the funeral?"

"Well…I believe I am, my good man. Look at my disguise!"

"Yeah, that's what I'm saying. It's a horrible costume."

"Well, it fooled you, didn't it? Gotcha, bitch! I went to the mall for breadsticks and left with a dope-ass disguise from the now-permanent Halloween shop. They were havin' a big sale, too. You know I can't pass up a good deal."

"You're getting too cocky, dude! You were carrying your own casket for Chrissake. *With Dave*, no less. You're trying to get caught!"

"Chill out, dude. Dave's an idiot. He rattled on and on for like fifteen minutes to me. I never said a word. He was just saying nice things to me via the casket. This has been an eye-opening experience. People say all sorts of stuff about you when you're dead. Lotta nice stuff. Lotta weird stuff. I've never seen half of these people. I had an old dude that *I do not know* tell me a story about me and him goin' fishing once. I've never been fishing in my life, dude. People are crazy! I'm loving it."

"You need to tighten up, dawg. You've gotta lay back. You're gonna blow it."

"Relax man. I'll chill out. What's the plan from here?"

"I have no idea," I confess. "But your casket's in the back of that haunted house hearse right now."

"Oh, shit!" he exclaimed. "That's the hearse from that haunted house where that kid went missing? That's so insane. Did you guys rent that? That's in poor taste, dude. I really hoped you guys would splurge for a hearse that isn't associated with an abandoned haunted house, but that's just me."

Just then, Kelsey approaches us. I haven't really gotten to talk to her since they got in. I have no idea what she knows or doesn't know at this point.

"Hey, Mic..." she says, double-taking at the strangely dressed Fischer. "Sorry to interrupt, but what's the plan?"

I don't think she recognizes Fish. She hasn't seen him in fifteen years, even if he weren't dressed like a flasher.[28]

"I'm not 100% sure..." I say, looking for Josh-Josh or Murphy—someone with a level head.

We're then approached by the brunch boys, our suckers in seersucker.

"Mic," says Pop. "How're we going to get up to the lake? What's the game plan?"

"Yeah, Mic," says Johnny. "Are we carpooling?"

"My mom let us drive Bertha over this mornin," says Ginger.

"You think she'd let us drive it up to the lake?" I ask.

---

[28] Strange beard, sunglasses, trench coat—if not a flasher, definitely some kind of pervert.

Bertha is Ronda's (Ginger's mother's) 70s Dodge conversion van. It's awesome. She's replaced the engine in this thing twice and refuses to give up on it despite rust and Bondo being the only things holding it together.

Ronda raced dirt bikes when she was a teenager and used Bertha to haul the bikes between competitions. Popular speculation is that Ginger was conceived in the back of this van. She (Bertha, not Ronda) can hold 8 people comfortably, and plenty more if you're willing to get creative. She's the perfect vehicle for transporting a group of friends between a fake wake and a phony funeral, as long as she can make it there and back.

"I'd think she'd let us take it up there," says Ging.

"You think it'll make it all the way?" asks Johnny. "She was shaking pretty good on the way here."

"She was just purring," says Pop. "Bertha loves stretchin' her legs. She was shaking 'cause she likes it…just like Rond…"

"I swear to God, dude. If you talk about my mom one more time, I'm gonna knock your teeth out of your fucking face," says Ginger.

"And rightfully so," says Kels.

"Thank you, Kelsey," says Ging, "but I think Bertha will make it. It doesn't seem like we have another good option."

"I mean…we could all just drive up separately. That way we know we'll get there," I say.

"Jesus, Mic. That's such a bitch move. What fun is that?" says Kelsey.

"Thank you, Kelsey," says Johnny. "Stop talking nonsense, Mic. We're in this together. We're a *family!*"

"Woo!" exclaims Murphy from 20 yards away. "Family, baby!"

"Yeah, Mic. Don't think so logically about this," says Pop.

"Yeah, Mic," says Ginger. "Don't put that negative energy on Bertha. She's seen more than you could hope to see in your entire life…Pop, if you say another fucking word about my mom…"

"What! *What?"* says Pop. "I wasn't going to say anything!"

"OK," says Johnny, "so, how're we getting the coffin up there?"

"Well…right now, it's in the back of that haunted house hearse," I say, at which point I realize that Fish is gone.

"Hey!" I say, concernedly. "Did you guys see what happened to that weird dude with the beard and the trench coat?"

"I saw that dude walking around the parade," said Ging.

"Yeah…who is that dude?" asks Johnny.

"Did you see where he went?" I ask.

"I haven't seen him since the parade," says Pop.

"What? He was standing right here when you guys came up to us. Right, Kels?"

"That pervy-looking dude?" asks Kelsey. "I don't know where he went. Who is he? Why are you stressing about it?"

All of the sudden, the horn on Josh-Josh's flower-covered tow truck starts beeping. (A comically high-pitched horn for such a big truck.) We turn towards it as the passenger door opens. It's Fish's mom holding a megaphone.

"Let's go, bitches!" she yells into the megaphone. "*Long live Fishy Fisherson*!"

She closes the door and Joshua's truck starts to round the back of the building.

"Oh, shit," says Doobs, who's found his way to us by now. "I think we're fuckin' leaving."

"Hey!" says Murphy. "Where's Dave?"

We look at Kelsey, who looks back at us with fear in her eyes. She pulls her phone out of her purse.

The engine of the hearse starts up and backfires, scaring the living shit out of us. It pulls away quickly, then stops abruptly.

The passenger door opens and out pops the head of our dear friend, Dave.

"*Long live Fishy Fisherson!*" he yells.

Then the hearse peels out of the gravel parking lot, spraying dust and melted snow at us.

"Oh, shit," says Kelsey. "We gotta go."

We all hustle to the van as other cars pull out behind the hearse. People are cheering and honking their horns. This is officially out of our control.

We all hop into Bertha. She smells like gasoline in a way that only boats and American cars from the 70s can.

Ginger is driving. I'm navigating, shotgun. In the very back, sitting on a pile of beanbag chairs, are Pop, Doobs, and Murphy. In front of them, on shag-covered captain's chairs, are Johnny and Kelsey. Those of us with seat belts strap in. The beanbag crew lights up a roach that they find sitting in an ashtray.

"Jesus, guys!" exclaims Ging. "Wait 'til we leave the parking lot. We've got police everywhere."

But the gang is too excited—riding on the high of a parade that's turned into what feels like a vehicular pursuit.

Bertha starts up. Thank the lord. We start to pull out of the parking lot and we're stopped by Meghan.

"Hey, Doobs! Did you guys take care of the tab?" asks Ging.

"For sure," he said. "Tracy knows what's going on. The place is spotless too."

"Yeah...it's amazing," says Murphy. "I definitely thought the place would be trashed. I remembered to grab the photo for the funeral, too." He holds up the giant framed monstrosity.

"Thank God," I say, rolling down the window.

"Meghan, thanks for all the help!" I say. "Tell your mom we'll be back to help clean up the parking lot. The hearse just peeled off and we've gotta catch up to them, stat!"

"Jesus. I'm coming with you guys," Meghan says.

"Oh, word?" I say.

Johnny slides open the side door.

"Come aboard, sailor," he says, jumping into the back with the rest of the guys.

Meghan sits down and closes the door.

"Yeah. If my uncle's driving the hearse, you guys are going to need all the help you can get."

"Wait, your uncle's driving the hearse?" asks Kelsey.

"Yeah," says Meghan, "and he's a horrible driver. Pretty sure he lost his license before I was born."

"Dave's in the hearse with him," says Kels.

"Why?" asks Meghan.

"I don't know. I think he got jazzed and must've wanted to ride close to the action."

“By ‘close to the action,’ do you mean ‘close to a dead body’?” asks Pop.

Kelsey laughs. “Yeah…that’s what I mean.”

“Well, let’s hope for the best,” says Meghan. “I’m sure they’ll be fine…probably. They’ll probably be fine.

SUNDAY SUNNY SUNDAE'S

Probably

As we enter the highway, Bertha seems to be purring quite nicely. It's about an hour and fifteen minutes to Port Clinton, our port for the ferry and jumping-off point for the funeral.

I didn't get the chance to talk to the Thompsons about funeral plans, and there's a large part of me that has very little faith in plans for the funeral existing at all, but I have chosen to temporarily leave my anxiety behind and let this day proceed as it may—partially for the sake of my sanity and partially because it seems we have no other choice.

The rest of the gang seems to be similarly calm. About fifteen minutes into the drive, we find ourselves sitting in the van, just listening to the Heart cassette that Ronda left in the stereo. "Magic Man" usually has the crew slammin', but today the squad just seems to let it wash over them. This is the first moment of ease we've had all day. Even Doobs seems relaxed. It's at this point, realizing we've let our guard down a bit, that I feel my anxiety creep back. I feel like I'm forgetting something.

We get off the interstate and hit State Route 12 when I realize that I need to call Uncle Rob, our man at the ferry. We're only forty-five minutes out, and I figure he'll need at least that much heads-up.

In the mid to late aughts, there was a concept introduced to the mobile phone market called the "ringback tone." Before the ringback tone, if you called someone, you'd hear the tone typically associated with waiting for someone to pick up a phone call, but if you had a ringback tone, every lucky person who had the pleasure of calling you would hear a song that you'd selected for them to hear, rather than the boring old ringing. Ideally, this would set the preverbal tone for the phone call—like an overture before a musical, but stupid.

The default ringback tone is the beginning of a MIDI version of Vivaldi's *Four Seasons*, entitled "Spring." You'll still hear this on occasion when calling your great-aunt on her birthday, but for the most part, the ringback tone is long out of fashion, used only by call centers, grandmothers, and weird dudes that still have a cell phone from 2008.

Both shockingly and unsurprisingly, Uncle Rob has a ringback tone. It's a verse and chorus from the Ringo Starr's "No-No Song."

A lady that I know just came from Colombia,

She smiled because I did not understand.

Then she held out some marijuana, uh huh,

She said it was the best in all the land.

No, No, No, No,

I don't smoke it no more.

I'm tired of waking up on the floor.

No, thank you, please, it only makes me sneeze,

And then it makes it hard to find the door.

As I realize what I'm hearing, I pause the cassette and turn on my speakerphone. This instantly awakens the sleepy van, as the "No No Song" is hype as hell.

Rob answers.

"Mr. Fox! I've been expecting your call. Your auntie sent me some pics of the parade. Looks raucous. I told the crew what was going down and they've been pre-gaming since. I don't say this lightly, but I'm jazzed, Kemosabe."

"Happy to hear it," I say to him. "Hey, we're about forty-five minutes out. I just wanted to give you a heads-up and make sure that we're still good to go."

"Don'tchuworryboutathing..." sings Rob, like a Stevie Wonder that's been sitting in the back of the fridge since last Christmas. "We got this, baby. It's gonna be great. The ferry's not even officially open yet. Y'all should be easy on, easy off, and the island should be pretty sleepy since we're not up and rollin' yet."

"That's great!" I say. "That's great."

As Rob starts giving me recommendations on what we should do on the island, we pass an old Dairy Dip on the side of the road. I remember stopping at this little ice cream spot as a kid. It's an old cinderblock building the color of cigarettes and lavender. It's nothing but a walk-up window and a few picnic tables out front, chained to a power pole. If you're going to get a shredded chicken sandwich, it might as well be from here, and I'd bet you can get hush puppies and a malt to go with that sandwich for no more than $3.50.

As I nostalgically hold the gaze of this magical little spot, I notice a car with its hood up behind the building, smoke billowing out of the engine compartment. Two men stand with their hands on their hips, pretending they know what they're looking at. One of these men is wearing well-tailored suit pants with his sleeves rolled up. The other is wearing a full-length fur coat.

"Goddammit," says Meghan.

"Hey, Rob!" I say to the phone. "I didn't catch any of that last bit. I'm going to have to call you back."

"What's the matter?" asks Kelsey.

"Well..." I say, trying to figure out if I've just seen what I think I saw.

"I think that was a hearse on fire back there," says Meghan.

I laugh. "It was not *on fire*."

"I saw that, too!" says Ging. "I think that was them."

"No way!" says Pop. "That'd be crazy."

I look at Ginger. He nods, waits for the next big county road intersection, and pulls the gnarliest U-turn I've ever been a part of.

"Jesus Christ!" yells Doobs. "I think the fuckin' wheels came off the ground."

"For sure," says Murphy. "I'm thrilled, but I have also soiled myself."

"Good girl," says Ginger, rubbing the dashboard. "Bertha knows what she's doin'. Dontchu fret!"

As we re-approach the Dairy Dip, we see the full silhouette of the hearse against the side of the purple building.

"So, what're the odds of it NOT being them?" wonders Johnny.

We laugh.

"This is so ridiculous," says Kelsey.

We park the van and the whole gang pours out the back.

"Hey guys!" says Dave, holding an ice cream cone. "What's up?"

"Hey, Dave! We were going to ask you the same thing," says Pop.

Dave laughs. "Oh, hey babe!" he waves awkwardly to Kelsey.

"Hey, dude! You can't just leave me at the fucking bar and peel out in some hearse with a weird dude wearing a fur coat."

"Oh, shit. Sorry, babe. I figured you'd want to ride with the homies. Thought I'd let you guys reminisce about old times. I assumed the van would be too crowded, so I decided to ride with this weird dude in the hearse. I was thinking about you, babe. But sorry I didn't run it by you, babe. I should've been more thoughtful, babe."

"Wellll…" she says dramatically, "when you put it like *that*."

"Jesus Christ…" says Pop, rolling his eyes.

Meghan walks over to her Uncle Donnie, who's staring at the smoking car.

"Hey, Donnie! What'd ya do?"

"Shit, Meg. I don't know."

"IhOhBaHeeDeh AnBoo AhKaKe," mumbles Dave with a mouth full of ice cream.

"What?" yells Meghan.

Dave takes another bite of ice cream. "IhBoo AhGaKeh."

"Are you saying 'bukkake?'" asks Johnny. "That's super gross, dude."

"No, no," says Dave with the ice cream again.

“Jesus,” says Doobs. “Wait ‘til you don’t have a mouth full of food. We are not savages, you fucking child.”

“Sorry,” says Dave, swallowing his ice cream. “It overheated and blew a gasket.”

“Bullshit,” says Pop. “You don’t know anything about cars.”

“Well, Mike…*you* tell us what happened, then!” yells Kels.

Pop laughs. “I don’t know anything about cars, either.”

“So, shut the fuck up!” says Ginger.

“How the fuck are we going to get this shit up to the lake now?” says Pop.

“I mean…we could just leave it,” says Johnny. “I mean it’s not like the hearse is really…”

Doobs looks at me, recognizing that Johnny Waterbottle is very possibly about to say that we should just leave the hearse because it’s not really doing anything other than transporting a casket full of peanut shells. Doobs has worked too fucking hard putting this whole thing together, just to let some seersucker-wearing yada-yada blow it.

So, he does the most subtle and tactful thing he can think of to change the subject. He tackles Johnny.

“Dammit, Doobs!” yells Johnny, stuck between the gravel parking lot and a 230lb 37-year-old man.

“Thank you, Jesus,” says Ginger, recognizing what just happened.

"Sorry, Johnny. I slipped," says Doobs, helping him up.

"You fucking tackled me!" cries Johnny, brushing off his seersucker pants.

"Oh, yeah…sorry I tackled you," says Doobs.

Murphy and I laugh.

"Get it together, Doobs," says Dave. "We've got to find another way to get Fish's body up to the lake."

Johnny's eyes go wide and his mouth falls open. He slowly lifts his head back, then nods slowly, looking at Doobs, finally realizing why he got tackled.

"Should we put it in the van?" asks Pop.

"Hell no," says Kelsey. "I'm not riding in the van with a *dead body*. And there's already eight of us in there, nine if you want to bring the dude in the fur coat."

"This fool's not riding in the van," says Meghan, pointing at Donnie. "That's why I'm here—to prevent the fruition of stupid ideas like that."

"C'mon, Meg!" says Donnie.

"No fucking way, dude," she replies.

"We could call a tow," says Ginger.

"Waaaay ahead of ya," says Murphy, hanging up his phone and pointing at the horizon.

We all turn and look off into the distance in a way that can only be done in the plains of the Southwest and the flats of the Midwest—where you can just barely make out the shape of something as it approaches.

And what do we see, blurred by the heat of the asphalt and the evaporating leftover snow?

A larger-than-life technicolored animal—changing shape as it approaches. Its colors swirl together and it seems to levitate, just above the ground. It moves towards us at increasing speed until we can finally see its full form—a tow truck covered, roof to rubber in flowers.

"Josh-Josh!" yells Dave.

—

An hour later, a casket full of peanut shells inside a broken-down hearse is riding on the back of a very elaborately decorated tow truck driven by Joshua Joshua and Fish's mother, Connie.

Meanwhile, the comfort limits of Bertha the Van are being pushed past capacity with the addition of Dave and Meghan's uncle, Donnie, who has decided that he should sit on top of a cooler between Ginger, who is driving, and myself, riding shotgun. He's turned around, facing the rest of the passengers, feet outstretched between Meghan and Kelsey, hands behind his head, leaning back onto the dashboard. The synthetic fibers of his imitation fur coat add a smell and essence to the van that, if bottled, could be sold as "Gas Leak Wet Basement."

He's really making himself at home, and it's an upsetting thing to see, as he is a foul human being.

Dave has taken root in the back of the van with the beanbag boys. He's shifting positions every few minutes in order to catch a view from every window in the van, like a dog on its first big car ride.

He's both nervous and excited, but he doesn't know why. This can be inferred from his body language and the giant smile on his face, but he's also saying things like, "I'm nervous and excited but I don't know why."

The gang's energy has been shifted. Anybody who was buzzed is now anxious. Anybody who was anxious is now exhausted. Anybody who was exhausted is even more exhausted. But Dave and Donnie seem to be doing just fine.

We're following closely behind the tow truck as Josh-Josh seems to be the only person who's got their shit together. We crest a couple overpasses north of Fremont and finally spot the beautiful waters of Lake Erie in all her murky glory. I call Rob at the ferry to let him know that we're about ten minutes away.

As we follow the tow truck off the exit, I see a man standing in front of a stop sign with his thumb out. We don't see too many hitchhikers these days, and honestly, I kinda miss it—not because I like to see someone trying to get somewhere who doesn't have the means to get there, but because it's nice to see someone willing to trust other people enough to get them where they're going—and this guy off our exit doesn't look down on his luck or anything. He has an overly manicured little beard, some sunglasses, and a plaid newsy hat like you'd see someone's retired father wear to an Irish pub or an open-mic…

"Goddammit," I say softly to myself.

"What?" says Ging.

I point to the little man. Who's now approaching the van with a cardboard sign that reads,

JUST LOOKIN 4 THE PARTY

Ginger, who hasn't seen Fish's stupid disguise yet, turns to me with crazy eyes and says, "Oh shit…is that…"

"Hey! It's that dude from the funeral!" exclaims Johnny Waterslide.

This alerts the rest of the van, including Dave, who immediately recognizes the strange little man as his fellow pallbearer.

"That's my guy right there!" says Dave, banging on the overly tinted windows of the van like a child who saw their friend outside the school bus.

Fischer gets right up on the window of the van so everyone can get a good look at him through the purple tint of the glass. Everyone seems to simultaneously come to the realization of what's happening, but Kelsey is the first to say something.

"No way," she exclaims softly.

I turn and look at the rest of the gang. Murphy is thrilled. Doobs is furious. Johnny and Popper are genuinely surprised. Then Donnie, in his flammable fur coat, reaches across my lap and rolls down my window. He then lays his disgusting body across mine to lean out and say,

"No room in this inn, amigo!" Donnie then reaches into his pocket and pulls out a wet, lukewarm, blue, plastic ice-pack that's shaped to contour three aluminum cans—like you'd see in your mother's freezer. He hands the ice-pack to the man and says, "Stay cool out there." Then rolls up the window.

Fischer looks at the ice-pack dumbfoundedly, then back up at me. He smiles a big smile through his fake-ass beard and walks up to the passenger door of the tow truck.

"What's he doin'?" asks Dave, now leaning over Donnie's rotting body to get a better look out the front window.

"Who knows," says Donnie. "You can't trust weirdos like that."

The door of the tow truck swings open and out jumps Connie. She gives the weird little man a big and extra-long hug. The little man turns to look back at us, gives us the finger, then the two of them hop into the truck.

The tow truck starts to drive off. I look at Ginger. He shakes his head, pushes Dave and Donnie out of the way, puts Bertha in gear, and off we go.

Meghan leans up behind my seat and drops her voice into a whisper.

“So was that…” she asks reluctantly.

“Yep,” I say.

“Got it,” she pauses. “And Dave doesn’t…”

“Right,” I say.

“Got it,” she pauses again. “So, is this a part of the plaaann?”

“There is no plan,” says Ginger.

“Right. Right…” she says. “Well, I think I’m up to speed.”

“As much as we can be,” says Kelsey.

“Great,” Meghan says.

—

As we drive through the small coastal towns of Northwest Ohio, there’s an overwhelming sense of nostalgia that fills the van. We pass pizza parlors and crummy old bars, ice cream huts, and greasy spoon breakfast-all-day style diners. We’ve all got memories of being up here with our families or friends from our childhood.

When most people think of “the coast,” they think of marinas and beaches, maybe a Ferris wheel on the pier. Or maybe they think of lighthouses and cliffs and lobsters on the dock.

And while the Lake Erie coast does have those things, it also has an overtly Midwestern quality. It’s not Midwesterny in the way that Chicago is, with its older city architecture, old-world culture, museum-heavy, touristy sort of thing. It's more like the rest of Ohio, but on the water.[29] [30]

If you've spent time in Cincinnati, there's a point where you've eaten a hotdog covered in Coney sauce buried under a pile of shredded cheese, and that was pretty nice, so why wouldn't you want that at the beach?

If you've spent time in Columbus, there's a point where you've had a giant pizza and a 30 rack of beer delivered to your house, and that was pretty nice, too, so why should being at the beach keep you from these nice things?

If you've spent time in Cleveland, there's a point where you've been out to a fancy restaurant and asked the waiter what the "catch of the day at market prices" was, despite the fact that you are hundreds of miles away from anywhere a saltwater fish could conceivably be caught. He then describes to you some fish from a place that you've never been, cooked in a way that you don't understand. You nod your head like you do understand because you're fancy and trying to impress your date. You reluctantly order it, despite the fact that your friend Randy told you to get the steak. Your date gets a massive salad with *grilled* instead of *fried* chicken (because she's being good). Your order shows up and you both make an audible noise to let the waiter and the

---

[29] Now...I must regress, as Cleveland and Cincinnati do share some of Chicago's old city architecture, old-world culture, museumy-ness. But I'm not talking about Northeast Ohio or Southwest Ohio. I'm talking about Northwest Ohio. Northeast and Southwest Ohio deserve their own books. And there are plenty of 'em out there, already. So I don't want to hear it. *ALRIGHT?!*

[30] I also don't want to hear any *"Aw man! But what about the Toledo Art Museum?! Toledo's got museums! Toledo's got culture! Fuck you, Mic..."* Listen...I know. But I'm telling a fuckin story, here! Let's move on. *Christ.*

people around you know that you're pleased with the gaudiness of the presentation. You don't notice that it's a different kind of fish than the one you ordered, because it's fish. You don't eat fish on the reg. Neither does your date. Both of you try it and act like you like it, but let's be honest, both of you would be happier with a burger from the spot up the road, so you end up going to that place for drinks after. You order a burger to split. You both comment on how sometimes a burger just hits the spot. You recognize that you're soulmates, get wasted, spend the night together, get married six months later, have a few kids, and live happily enough for the rest of your days. So, why should the fact that you're at the beach keep you from fulfilling your destiny?

People up here know what they like. And even if they're on vacation, they don't need to feel like they're in some far-off land, experiencing wild new things. They just want the joy that comes from a different view, the excitement in knowing that they don't have work tomorrow, and the comfort in knowing that they can still have all the food and TV that they enjoy on the daily, right here by the water.

As a kid, you cast judgement, easily. You tell yourself, "I'm not gonna do it like this. I'm gonna do something cooler. Yeah, my life's gonna be wild." But as you get older, after you scratch that adventure bug a few times, there's a point where you look back at those sleepy times at the lake with fondness, and once you can feel that fondness, it's not long before you find yourself scheduling a yearly sleepy retreat, with no plans wilder than taking a nap on the couch before you go back to the same little pizza pub for dinner. Cap that pizza with a little walk on the beach. Maybe go back to that other little hole-in-the-wall for a beer, a little karaoke, another beer, and a walk back to the condo.

I'm tearing up just thinking about it.

—

Filled with nostalgia, we follow Josh-Josh's truck into the gravel parking lot of the ferry's shipyard. I haven't been here in nearly a decade, but from the looks of it, not much has changed. Some things've gotten a new coat of paint, but if it ain't broke, why you tryin' to make it fancy? Fancy's for fools.

To our surprise, the grounds of the dock are pretty lively, despite the fact that the ferry isn't open yet. Joshua's flower-covered tow truck is approached by a man wearing a hi-vis-construction-vest-colored PFG fishing shirt and a white visor. They dialogue for a second, and the man gives him a couple of directions with his hands. I assume we should follow Josh-Josh, but the man signals for us to turn left.

I roll down my window and before I can say anything, he asks, "You guys here for the funeral?"

I nod.

"Well, head up that hill and park with the rest of the cars."

"Rest of the cars?" I ask.

He laughs. "*Yah*," he replies with a bit more sass than I would've expected. "Hey, are you Fox? You Rob's nephew or somethin'?"

I laugh. "I am. I mean, he's not really my…yeah…I guess he's my uncle."

“Well, I’m sorry to hear that.” He laughs so hard that he starts into a coughing fit. He recomposes himself. “Just go park up that hill and walk down to the boat.”

We park in a small lot with around 15 other cars and file out of the van and onto the gravel. As we start walking towards the boat, we begin to start naturally moving in twos. Big funeral vibes. But instead of processing through an aisle of a church, we’re weaving through the narrow spaces between boats sitting parked on their trailers. There’s some light chatter, but for the most part, the gang is quiet and curious as to what happens next.

Because it’s off-season, the parking lot of the dock is being used as private boat storage—a killer side hustle, really. It’s like a makeshift outdoor maritime museum. Cigarette boats from the 80s and giant fishing boats from the 40s, beautiful old sailboats from the 60s and strange one-of-a-kind houseboats from who knows when, all sitting on their trailers, parked comically (and very impressively) close together. Some are covered, some are not. And none of us corn-fed fools would think about it one way or the other.

As we exit the maritime maze, we find ourselves standing at the water, looking up at the ferry in all her blue sunburnt glory. We take a moment and look at each other, realizing that most of us hadn’t been on a boat this big in a long time. On top of that, none of us have a plan regarding the funeral or the rest of the day for that matter.

The high from the parade has officially worn off and we now collectively settle into the reality that is upon us.

All of us, except for Dave, who is seemingly high-as-hell from whatever Johnny Wonderwall was passing around in the back of the van.

"Hey, Mickey," says Meghan quietly, "is there a plan from here or are we just kinda going with the flow?"

I nod and return from my daze.

"Where's Josh-Josh?" I say.

"Who's Josh-Josh?" she asks.

"What?" Responds Murph. "The dude with the tow truck, Meghan. *Keep up!"*

"How'd we lose him?" asks Doobs. "He's driving a tow truck covered in flowers.

Then we hear, from a loudspeaker on a phone pole at the end of the dock, in a basketball starting lineup voice, "Ladies and gentlemen…this is your *captain* speaking."

"He's not the captain," says another, more nasally voice, also coming from the P.A.

"Well, technically I'm not *the* captain. But I *am* the Party Captain," says the first voice.

"I don't care," says the nasally voice.

"And as Party Captain," continues the first voice, "I'd like to welcome you to the Lake Erie Fun-Filled Funeral Ferry!"

"Jesus Christ," says Doobs. "This is too much."

"Awesome," Dave whispers to himself in awe.

The three amigos in seersucker, along with Kelsey and Meghan, are equally as thrilled, judging by the stupid matching grins plastered across their faces.

Our attention is then shifted to a group of people leaning over the edge of the boat. Waving down at us from 20 feet in the air are Fish's mother, between six and eight other members of Fish's family, Joshua Joshua, and the Thompson twins.

"Goddamn," says Murphy, "I forgot about the Thompson twins. I hadn't thought about the Thompson twins for the entire ride up here. I miss *not* thinking about them."

"Never forget," says Johnny as he starts into another Thompson Twins song.

"All aboard!" shouts the nasally voice from the other end of the boat. We scurry in our formalwear over to the switchbacks of boat ramps. As we board the vessel, we're greeted by Josh-Josh and my dear old, and now extra-extra-large, Uncle Rob.

The Uncle Rob of my childhood was a slim interpretive dancer type. In the 90s he put off major malnourished, self-proclaimed visionary, post-homeless vegan energy. He had a snake, for Chrissake.

But the Uncle Rob we see before us is no longer a loose-fitting, moth-eaten, semi-transparent men's medium, but a full-blown XXXL fishing-shirt-with-the-vents-in-it character who somehow emanates the exact same energy as his smaller self.

"Mr. Fox!" he says, bear-hugging me off my feet.

"Great to see you, Rob. Thanks again for hooking this up."

"You got it, big dog. How're your folks? How's ya mutha?" he asks, turning on a strange New England accent for no reason at all.[31]

"The family's good, Rob. Everybody sends their love."

"Yeah. I know," says Rob. "They're already on the boat. We've all just been waiting for your stony asses to show up with this stupid coffin."

"What?" I ask, looking over Rob's shoulder to see my brother and dad waving at me with big stupid grins on their faces.

---

[31] People from Northwestern Ohio are kind of known for having no accent when they speak, and because we don't have a local dialect to push to the side, a lot of us are able to shift in and out of strange vocal inflections with ease. The exploration of both foreign and domestic accents, along with their corresponding subcultures, begins the moment we're placed in front of a television, and thanks to the amount of television we consume, our minds have the room to study these vocal and behavioral tendencies, without pause, for years at a time.

The ability to speak confidently and effectively with panache is a valuable party trick as a child and a great way to get into trouble as an adolescent, but left unchecked, the practice of sliding in and out of different manners of speaking continues well into adulthood and is usually only stopped once you subconsciously slip into an ill-timed accent—at the wrong place, at the wrong time, in front of the wrong people.

But, luckily for us, there's a safe and very effective way to keep yourself out of these sticky situations: only speak and associate with other people who also grew up in Northwest Ohio—that way, you'll never be embarrassed or called out in public or punched in the face for speaking to someone in the wrong way. This practice of isolating oneself in a group of similarly experienced people is common in many parts of the world, but it's Northwest Ohio where you'll find this at its finest.

My mother and Connie stand beside them, just chatting it up like they're at the salon. (Lots of hand gestures and laughing.)

"Jesus, Mic," says Doobs. "We've gotten this far, and now your family's here to blow the whole thing wide open?"

My family is notorious for not being able to keep a secret, so I understand Doobs's concern.

But now is not the time for fear.

"Sorry, Doobs. They'll behave, I promise."

"They'll behave like a bunch of fuckin' fools is what they'll fuckin' do!"

"Easy, Doobs," says Murphy. "*Eeeeasy.*"

"Yo Mic," says Johnny Waterslide, "where's your sister?"

He turns and looks at Dave, then back at me. Then Dave turns, looks at me, then at his shoes, then at my mother, then back at me, then back at his shoes.

"Which sister?" I ask slowly.

"I don't know..." he says stupidly and directly at Dave, "either of 'em." [32]

---

[32] This line of dialog is directly referencing a bit from earlier where we establish that Dave is the dumb-dumb who was convinced that my obviously-adopted sister was actually a love child brought into this world

The horn from the boat sounds again. Party Captain Rob rings the bell and now we're riding on a big-ass boat, heading for Put-in-Bay, Ohio.

We all begin to find our way around to the bow of the ferry. This particular boat is a 140ft monster that can handle 300 people and a dozen cars on a good day, but today, as we walk around to the big nose of the boat, it's just 20–30 people and a broken-down hearse holding a casket full of peanut shells.

I hug my family, then survey the rest of the boat.

The Fischers and some other family friends that I don't know are chatting quite jovially amongst themselves, putting off real cocktail hour energy. It would be strange if it *were* a real funeral, but it's not and we're on a boat now, so who am I to tell them to pipe down.

The Thompson twins are handing out business cards to Josh-Josh, Johnny Wonderwall, Ginger, and Murphy. Doobs is pacing around the bathrooms. He does get motion sickness, but from the looks of it, he probably just has to go pee. Meghan, Kelsey, and Pop are hanging on the starboard side, chatting quietly and politely. This would be appropriate behavior if this were a *real* funeral, but it's not, so it makes me a little nervous.

Donnie, who I'd forgotten about for a second, appears out of thin air in his faux fur coat, opens the door to the hearse, pulls out a pack of Virginia Slims, and hops up onto the hood. (And while it is his car, I'd like to make it perfectly

---

through a scandalous affair between my freckle-faced mother and a small black man from Toledo.

clear, that he *is* a monster for sitting on the hood of a hearse while there's a supposed body inside.) Dave hops up onto the hood with him. They sit there, leaning back on the windshield like Wayne and Garth watching airplanes pass overhead. Both of them blissed-out, smoking Virginia Slims like a couple freaks. Monsters attract monsters. Like attracts like. I'm not a scientist, but someone's written about this, I'm certain of it.

I see Kelsey notice Dave's behavior, become upset, recompose herself, then turn around, looking out at the water. Pop and Meghan turn towards her, then out towards the water, themselves. The three of them lean on the railing of the boat, just talking. The mood gets heavy.

"So…Kelsey and Dave are engaged?" asks my brother.

"Yeah," I say.

"Well…these aren't the vibes. *Right?*"

"Right. Those vibes haven't really been vibing today."

"Well…you've gotta go figure that out, dude."

"What? Why? That's not really my business, dude."

"Well," he says, "you're the fuckin fools who put Dave in this situation. If you guys didn't throw this elaborate, and may I say, *impressive* fake-ass funeral, he wouldn't be sitting on that hearse with that weird guy smoking those old lady cigarettes while his fiancée exponentially loses respect for him."

Damn, Brother's right. This whole fucking thing is just an elaborate ruse to skip Dave's bachelor party, and instead of just messing with him a little bit, we sent him spiraling into his old ways. He's backsliding into the character that we've cast him as.

None of us have seen him in years, but the last time we did, he had battened down the hatches, nose to the grindstone. He was going to leave his carefree, 30-year-old teenage ways behind and be a better version of himself. Sure, we gave him shit for going out west, *again*, but at least he was doing something. At least he had his head on straight. Hell, he must've done a pretty good job getting his shit together, because he got the homie, Kelsey, to agree to marry his stupid ass.

But look at him now, I haven't seen him and Kelsey talk at all, not once since they got to the bar. I haven't seen any chemistry, either. He jumped right back into the role of the court jester for his high school buddies. Everybody does that to an extent, but seeing Kelsey react to his old behaviors feels especially bad. They had a good life going out west. They'd gotten their shit together. She was a fitness influencer or some shit and he was some kind of mortgage loan officer or something. Personally, that sounds like a horrible time, but they were making it work. And they were happy together, and now look at them! Jesus! We ruined it! They've got kids, for Chrissake!

"What are you talking about?!" says my brother.

"What?" I ask, waking up out of my daze.

He laughs. "They don't have kids."

"What? Who?"

"Dave and Kelsey. You just said 'And now look at em! Jesus! We ruined it! They've got kids for Chrissake!' They don't have kids, dude. Relax. You're making stuff up in your head again. Just fix it. I'm sure everything's fine. You've just gotta stop encouraging him to act like a 19-year-old dumbass."

"What should I do?"

"I don't know. Do less, I guess. Go talk to Kelsey. Keep Popper from trying to put the moves on her. You know that dude's gonna try to swoop in and snatch her up like a fuckin' 90s movie."

"Shit. You're right. We can't let our bullshit split up the family."

"They've got kids for Chrissake," he says.

I laugh. "Right!"

I head over to where Meghan, Kelsey, and Pop are standing, leaning on the railing of the deck. Popper's speaking attentively.[33]

"I mean, what do you want me to do? You want me to say something to him? I'm sorry he's acting like a selfish idiot,

---

[33] It's like *listening* attentively, but narcissistic.

Kelsey. But he *is* a selfish idiot," Popper says, just loud enough to hear over the water.

"Shut the fuck up, Pop," says Kelsey. "You've got no clue what you're talking about. And hell," she says, laughing, "look at you in your high water seersucker. Antebellum-Pee-Wee-Herman-lookin' ass! Trying to talk to me about Dave being the selfish idiot. You fucking dumb-dumbs were so selfish that you couldn't even throw a normal bachelor party for your buddy. You had to throw a fake funeral instead. You couldn't handle your buddy being happy. You *had* to make it about yourself."

"Jesus, Kels. Tell us how you really feel," says Pop, begging for Kelsey to slap him.

"Kelsey…" I say, trying to chime in.

"Shut the fuck up, Mic. This is your fault too."

"Well, I just think—"

Pop waves his hand back and forth across his neck, telling me to drop it. I do.

Then I don't.

"Listen, Kelsey, I'm sorry the day has gotten a little out of control—"

"Shut up, Mic! You can't fix everything, all right! You can't."

"Sorry."

Kelsey pauses and looks down at her shoes.

“I guess…” she says, holding back tears. “I guess this trip has been an eye-opener.

She pauses again.

“I guess I just thought Dave had changed. I thought he’d grown out of this kinda thing. But he hasn’t looked at me once since we got out of the car at the wake. He’s just peacocking for you guys. It’s like he doesn’t even remember that I’m here. It’s like he doesn’t even remember that this is supposed to be a funeral. He’s just hanging with the guys, being the idiot you expect him to be. It’s a self-fulfilling prophecy with you assholes. It always is. I mean, look at him. He’s smoking old lady cigarettes on the hood of that broken-down hearse with that weird pervy guy. Living his best life.”

She pauses again as the four of us turn to look at these two freaks sitting on this busted car.

“I mean, *look* at him.” She says, pointing. “That’s his future, sitting right next to him. Just a couple gross weirdos getting their kicks, no fucks to be given.”

Popper laughs. “It’s kinda beautiful in a way.”

Kelsey covers her mouth with her hand and walks briskly towards the bathroom, trying to hold back tears.

“You guys are fucked up,” says Meghan. “I hardly know you guys, but you’re obviously fucked up.”

Meghan follows Kelsey to the bathroom.

“Jesus, Pop! What the fuck!?” I exclaim.

“What?” he says, pretending he doesn’t feel as bad as he obviously does. “I’m just saying what everyone else is thinking.”

“What are you fucking talking about?!” I yell over the waves. “The only thing you were thinking about is how to kick Dave to the curb so you could sweep Kelsey up like a wounded pup. Classy stuff, Pop.”

He looks down at his feet.

“This was *not* a part of the plan,” I say, breaking the silence.

“What fucking plan?” says Popper. “This whole day has been a goddamn shit show!”

“Well, that doesn’t mean you have to go around trying to fuck it up for our homies. You don’t have to ruin people’s lives.”

“Listen, man, Kelsey’s my friend. So is Dave. But do you think those two should be getting married? Maybe we’re doing them a favor. Hell, she said it—maybe this trip’s *supposed* to be an eye-opener.”

“Fuck you, Pop.”

“Fuck you, Mic.”

We go our separate ways. I walk towards the bathrooms, hoping that I *can* be but also hoping that I don’t *have* to be the one to deescalate this situation.

I take a corner too hot and physically bump into Doobs in his pinstripe-and-paisley tuxedo.

"Oh shit. Sorry, Doobs."

"Hey, Mic. Just the guy I wanted to see. What the *fuck* is going on? I just saw Kelsey run into the bathroom crying, Meghan from the bar following her."

"Yeah, dude. Which way'd they go?"

"You can't go into the women's restroom, Mic. *This* is Ohio. There are rules. You can't just go moseying into the ladies' room like you can out in California. This is a civilized society."

Just then, the women's room door opens, and out emerges a shorter man with a dark pointy beard wearing sunglasses and a plaid newsy hat.

The three of us stand there in front of the bathroom door, staring at each other. Doobs looks at the man, then back at me, then back at the man. The man follows the same pattern: looking right at Doobs, then at me, then back at Doobs.

"That's the stupidest disguise I have ever seen," Doobs says to Fischer, calmly.

"Thank you, my good man," Fish says, bowing to Doobs.

They both look back at me, then back at each other.

"Did you procure it at the now-permanent Halloween store in the mall?" Doobs asks.

"Certainly," Fish responds. "And where by chance do you procure a giant pinstripe tuxedo with tails and..." Doobs opens his jacket to reveal the interior, “paisley lining?” finishes Fish, acknowledging the outrageousness of what he’s seeing.

“Well, if you must know,” says Doobs calmly and confidently, “I got it at the tuxedo shop next to that Halloween store in the mall.”

“It’s beautiful!” says Fischer. “And there’s no vomit on it or anything. I hope you kept the receipts.”

“Thank you, my good man. And you *know* that I kept the receipts. I’m keeping all the pockets stitched up on the jacket too. It’s super annoying, but lucky for me the pockets on the pants go all the way down to the knees!” Doobs says, placing his hands and most of his forearm into the giant pockets.

“That is really something!” Fischer says.

All of a sudden, the three of us get knocked to the ground by someone flying around the corner.

“Oh shit! Sorry guys.” Says Dave, reaching his hand out to help me up.

Doobs and I look at each other, then at the stupidly dressed Fischer, then up at Dave.

“My bad, guys. Comin in a little too hot,” he says, as Doobs stands and brushes his suit off.

Dave reaches his hand out to lift Fischer up off the ground. Fischer reluctantly gives his hand back.

"Hey, I like that hat!" says Dave, gesturing to Fish's stupid plaid newsy.

"Thaaank you," says Fish in a horribly strange, almost *Gollum from the Lord of the Rings*-ish way.

We all stand in silence, awkwardly looking at each other, waiting for the other shoe to drop.

"OK..." says Dave, "have you guys seen Kelsey? I haven't seen her in a sec. I feel like I probably got a little too blitzed in the van and fucked something up."

"I saw her and Meg go into the bathroom a little bit ago," says Doobs, "but I wouldn't go in there if I were you. *This* is Ohio. There are rules. You can't just go moseying into the ladies' room like you can out in California. This is a civilized society."

"Fuck you, Doobs," Dave says, running into the bathroom.

The three of us stand there in silence for a second.

"What the fuck was that?" I exclaim.

"I don't know," says Fish. "That interaction felt too close. Like, how does he not know it's me? Is he really dumb? I mean, I know he's stupid. But, like...is he *really* stupid?"

"I guess so," says Doobs, "but I think modulating your voice so it sounds like a gremlin on Quaaludes really added to the disguise."

"Yeah, man...that voice was something. You gonna keep up with that?" I ask.

"Trust the process," says Fish. "I'm exploring this character live. It's called improvisation. Ever heard of it?"

"Yeah, you're a real Wayne Brady."

Ding ding...Ding ding...Ding ding.

The ferry's bell rings, and the three of us wander up to the deck.

"Hey, Fish, maybe find somewhere inconspicuous to camp out until we get to the island," I say. "Your outfit really draws a lot of attention, and I don't think the rest of the guys will be able to contain themselves if you start hanging out like it's no big deal. They've been drinking and smoking doinks all day, and I don't think we need to rock the boat until we're on solid ground."

"Mic's right," says Doobs, "and you know I hate to say that. I also would like to go on the record and say that using the term 'rock the boat' on a boat is very upsetting."

"Yeah, fuck you, Mic," says Fish.

"My apologies," I say, bowing.

"But I get it," says Fish. "I'll be up in the crow's nest if you need me."

"Crow's nest!" laughs Doobs.

"Like it's a fucking pirate ship!" I say.

"Listen, I'll be in whatever the equivalent of a crow's nest is if you need me," says Fish, "but you fools need to clean up whatever this mess is between Dave and Kelsey."

Fish makes a comically dramatic exit, like a villain in a Bollywood movie. As soon as he's out of sight, Kelsey and Dave come up the stairs and meet us on the main deck. Kelsey avoids eye contact and cruises right past us. Dave just stands beside us, silently.

"You guys all right?" I ask, reluctantly.

Dave looks at me with a blank facial expression and his eyes full to the brim with tears. Then he walks away.

"Goddammit!" says Doobs. "What the fuck happened, Mic?"

Our eyes follow Dave as he walks along the taffrail to the front of the boat, where the rest of the gang is standing, cutting up. Kelsey stands on the starboard side, talking to Fish's mom.

"Dammit, Mic!" Doobs says again.

The bell of the boat rings again.

"*Land hooo!*" yells Uncle Rob from the upper deck of the boat, holding a telescope. It's funny because you can see land the whole time. It's not like we're out to sea or anything. We're on a 20-minute ferry ride to an island that you can see from the mainland. But when Rob yells, "Land hooo!" he means, "Hey! We're here!"

And he's right.

41.6542° N, 82.8207° W

Here we are. Docking on the south end of South Bass Island, home of Put-in-Bay, Ohio.

I really didn't want to get specific regarding the names of towns in this book. If you've got a map of Southeastern Michigan or Northwestern Ohio, you can probably deduce or infer where I'm from and where we're heading, etc.

And while I'm more than happy being vague about the specifics of my hometown (especially because many of the details are fictional), there's no way to frame the town of Put-in-Bay as anything other than what it is.

South Bass Island is a five-and-a-half-square-mile rock 35 miles east of Toledo and 14 miles northwest of Sandusky. Of the three Bass Islands on Lake Erie, it is the southernmost. It's home to 630ish residents—a majority of whom live in the larger, unincorporated chunk of the island. The rest of the residents live three miles up the road in Put-in-Bay.

Put-in-Bay is home to some 140 people. It has one school, one bank, one grocery store, one hardware store, one airport, no hospital, and 25 bars. If I were to describe it to someone who's never been, I'd say it's a realization of MTV's Spring Break programming, but everyone is 15-20 years older and 15-20 lbs heavier than what Viacom was selling to the youth of the late 90s.

Lil Jon and the East Side Boyz play back to back with Kenny Chesney at the motel pool's booty-shaking extravaganza. Jimmy Buffet rolls right into Three 6 Mafia without question or concern at the bar's wet T-shirt contest. Behavior that's been written off as politically incorrect 10 years earlier now reigns supreme, with no checks or balances other than that of the reggae air horn sound coming from the DJ's 2010 MacBook.

To a more discerning population, this description may sound vile. But if the Democratic Party encouraged critical thinking rather than quick disgust, some of us would be able to take a step back and see this place for what it truly is: a purely unpretentious place, for better or worse.

The real beauty of Put-in-Bay is that no one who sets foot on this island is attempting to have or create anything other than a great time for everyone else on this island. It's true chaotic-neutral. It's a beautiful cross-section of western society's *Greatest Hits.* There's something for everyone on Put-in-Bay. It appeals to the lowest common denominator of our modern existence.

Now, that statement probably further pushes coastal elites, who haven't yet closed this book, into questioning why they're still here. Why on earth would anyone want to appeal to the lowest common denominator of people? The lowest common denominator of people is animalistic! Why is it good or even acceptable that people stoop to the level of their animalistic tendencies? And I can see your argument. I agree. People shouldn't primarily exist in this animalistic state. People shouldn't enter the thunder dome *full time.* However, Put-in-Bay is for vacation. Vacation should be a break from reasonable times. Put-in-Bay is just for fun. Wouldn't you like to have fun?

"Of course!" you say. "But I have plenty of fun on my vacations and I never have to see a large 40-year-old white woman competitively shake her ass to a mash-up of "Moves Like Jagger" and Usher's "Yeah."

Touché. But think about your vacation for a second. It was great, right? You stayed at the cool little boutique hotel. You didn't realize that it didn't *really* have an elevator, so you lugged all your bags up four floors. It was worth the exercise! Then you got dressed and went out to a nice-ass restaurant that you could only get into at 4:30. You guys were all excited about it and you made your reservations months in advance and shit. Then you got there and the server was having a bad night, and the food was pretty good, but they were out of the appetizer that your friend said "you just *have* to have!" Then you saw them bring that app out to some other table, but you blew it off like it was no big deal, enjoyed the meal enough, paid for it like it was *definitely* worth it, and tipped big because you want them to know that you're a big dog.

You went to that new weirdo art museum that you read about online, and it was great because they were showing this sculptor that you've seen before. You got to talking with the gallery manager and things were going great, but then you mispronounced the artist's name and she corrected you. You blew it off, but it stung a little and you thought about it later on.

Then you went to the late showing of the new comedically Brechtian spin on *Mamma Mia!*, which might have been good if not for the fact that it was *so bad*. There was no fucking music in it and the lady next to you sneezed all over your new sweater.

I'm sure there were good parts to that vacation as well, but those are the parts I remember hearing about. Yes, you experienced some times with some artistic merit, and that's all well and good…right?

But hear me out. Close your eyes and imagine this:

You go on vacation…

No one around you is trying to do or make anything of artistic or cultural value. In fact, they're all *exclusively* having the best time they've ever had, so much so that not one of these people is even close to considering how they could be perceived by any other being in the entire world.

When's the last time that *you* were not even remotely concerned about what other people thought of you? Doesn't that sound kind of nice?

"They'd find me out in a second!" you say. "Those animals would sniff my liberal ass out in no time at all! I wouldn't feel comfortable. I wouldn't be able to let my guard down. And why would I even *want* to let my guard down around those people? Look at them! Shaking their asses to Nelly! What fucking year is it?"

HEY! Relax. Take a breath.

You're right. If I showed those rednecks what your bougie-ass just said, they'd be pissed…but that's why Trump was elected—not because these fools are hateful bigots, but because people like you talk down to them and view them as incompetent, simple-minded animals. They elected that dude to spite your ass. And they will keep electing fools and implementing chaotic policy until you meet them at their level and acknowledge them for what they're good at—having a drunk-ass, rip-roaring good time in the middle of nowhere without any help or influence from pretentious culture vultures.

We can all learn from each other. We can all use a lesson on critical thinking and comprehending all sides of an argument, and we can all take a breath and stop repeating bullshit that our loudest buddy's been spewing from his shit-eating lips.

Sorry. I yield my time.

I'd like to invite you to drop your preconceived notions and your pretentious nature to join us on an island 35 miles east of Toledo, 14 miles northwest of Sandusky—a place near and dear to the hearts of anyone who's fully embraced its true chaos—Put-in-Bay, Ohio.

BICYCLE RENTALS
BY TOMMIE

Golf Carts and Caskets

While you *can* put a car on the ferry, and people who live on South Bass Island *do* own and operate motor vehicles, the major modes of transportation for tourists on Put-in-Bay are bicycles and golf carts. These are also, in my opinion, two of the funnest and most ridiculous modes of transportation. And while I was and still am concerned about the seemingly bad state of my dear friends' relationship, I do feel distracted by the giddiness I feel seeing the gang peruse the selection of alternative transportation choices that the vendors of South Bass Island present as soon as you get off the ferry.

Any other time I've been to Put-in-Bay, the selection of golf carts and bicycles has been slim pickings. I've only ever been to the island during peak tourist season, and usually, when I get off the boat, the only golf cart available is a pretty gnarly situation with a questionable paint job and some poor high school kid on summer break cleaning vomit off of the seat.

But today was different. Without the ferries dropping a few hundred tourists off each hour, the golf carts were lined up for blocks. Every little rental situation had a full fleet of carts, ready to roll. The gang's eyes light up.

Watching a group of grown men ogle over a fleet of electric go-carts is like watching a group of kids at an ice cream shop. The magic! The possibilities! The simple joy! The wonder of it all!

Watching those same grown men realize that the golf cart rental shops are closed *because* the ferries aren't bringing thousands of people to the island yet is like watching those same kids walk out of that ice cream shop, empty-handed, just to be shat on by some seagulls.

"Mother fucker," says Ginger. "All the rental spots are closed?!"

"God Dammit," says Johnny Waterbottle. "All I wanted was to drive a golf cart to a funeral. That's the only reason I even came to this stupid thing."

"Same, dude. Same," says Pop.

A collective groan rolls through the crowd as everybody realizes our oversight.

The group seems to split up, survival-instinct-style, in search of an open golf cart rental.

"We could all pile in the hearse?" says Dave. "It's pretty roomy in there."

Kelsey, Fischer's mother, and I turn and look at him like he's a sick weirdo (which he certainly is, I might add.)

"Didn't that thing break down on the way here?" asks Connie.

"Yeah," I reply, turning my attention to the disturbing old wagon. "How'd it even end up on the boat?"

"It just started right up for me," says Josh-Josh.

"What?"

"Yeah. I thought the same thing, but when I was pulling it off the truck, I thought, 'Well, how're we gonna get this thing on the damn boat?' So I tried starting it up. It seemed all right, so I drove it up onto the ferry."

"Unbelievable," says Kelsey.

"I know!" says Josh-Josh.

"No. I mean, look at that thing," Kelsey says, pointing.

We turn and look to see Donnie driving the hearse off the boat, the car making concerning dry heaving sounds.

"That doesn't sound *greeeeat*," says Murphy.

"Yeah. It's definitely not great," agrees Josh-Josh.

The hearse approaches us and eventually stops. Donnie jumps out.

"She lives!" he cries triumphantly. "They don't build 'em like this anymore."

"That's true," says Meghan, "but I'm not riding in the damn hearse with Donnie. One of you assholes knows *somebody* who can rent us some bicycles or something."

The group collectively takes a pause and thinks. Then we turn to hear the sound of jingling keys and a little bell ringing against a shop door.

"Tammie?" says Connie, questioningly, as a very tan and wild-looking woman opens the door to a little bike rental shop.

"Aunt Tommie! I told you we were going to make it a surprise!" says Tyler Thompson.

"I am so sorry," the woman says. "Are you Connie?" she asks, shaking Connie's hand. "I'm Tommie Thompson, I'm Tammie's younger and more attractive twin sister."[34]

"We were going to make 'em sweat, Aunt Tommie! You blew it!" says Travis Thompson, with the tone of a whining child.

"Well, you boys need to be nicer to your friends. They've had a long, *hard* day," says Tommie Thompson in an upsettingly gross way.

"Connie…I am so sorry for your loss," she says, hugging Connie's face tightly against her outrageously over-the-top boob job.

"Thank you," says Connie. "That means a lot."

"Well, I've heard you guys need to get to a funeral at the monument?!"

She pauses as if we're going to respond in a way that a motivational speaker would want a group of 3rd graders to

---

[34] As you may remember, Tommie is the sister to Tammie Thompson, mother of Tyler and Travis Thompson. Tammie was the one running the Toledo tech scheme that got busted because she couldn't stop talking about her twin sister, Tommie. This is *that* twin sister, Tommie.

respond to an "I can't *hear youuuu!"* at the start of some sort of field day situation.

"Well, you've come to the right place!" she exclaims, pointing at the sign above her shop.

BICYCLE RENTALS BY TOMMIE

"Yeah, guys..." says Travis, "So basically, as a gift to the grieving family of our dear old comrade, Arthur Fischer," he says, pausing to acknowledge Connie and the rest of the family, "we've rented out Aunt Tommie's bicycle fleet so we can get to the lighthouse."

"I guess Donnie's going to meet us there in the hearse?" says Tyler, gesturing to Donnie. Donnie isn't paying attention at all. In fact, he appears to be on the phone with some *strange.*[35]

There's another awkward pause as if we're all going to cheer for the Thompson twins.

"OK, well...I guess we should get goin?" says Johnny reluctantly.

"Yeah!" says Connie. "It's time to go."

---

[35] Based purely on body language and hushed little phrases like, "You'd like that wouldn't you. I mean, I've gotta do this funeral thing, but I'll probably be here for the rest of the night if you're free."

Here we find ourselves, the whole damn funeral party, maybe twenty-five people, some of whom haven't ridden a bicycle in decades, deciding to take a self-guided three-mile bicycle tour of South Bass Island: from the rental depots on the southern side of the island to Perry's Victory and International Peace Memorial on the northern side of the island.

I fully expect this to end in disaster, especially since half of these fools think a tandem bicycle is the way to go.[36]

But despite my reservations, things go pretty smoothly. The smiles on the faces of people who don't regularly ride bicycles are truly a sight to behold. It's beautiful. If you could bottle it and drink it through a crazy straw, it would end wars; it would build bridges; it would cure diseases.

The only tough part of this otherwise beautiful moment is that Dave and Kelsey don't seem to be speaking at all. Kelsey appears to be in a decent enough mood, despite present circumstances. She's riding a tandem with Meghan, someone she hadn't met until this morning, and Dave seems to be keeping his distance in the back of the pack, on a gold glitter banana-seat bike that appears to be sized for a swaggy 13-year-old rather than a dude pushing 6'4" and 40 years old.

---

[36] For the record, I think tandem bicycles are mad dangerous. Unless the two riders are experienced and really in sync, bicycles built for two are bicycles heading to the hospital (something this island is lacking entirely). Someone once told me that the true test of a relationship sits somewhere between the tandem bicycle and the canoe trip. There's some truth there. In regards to our current situation, I'd take the canoe over the tandem any day. But alas.

Meghan and I seem to be the only characters that are even slightly concerned about this grift. I know it's not really my business, but I do feel partly responsible for putting them in this situation. Popper may feel a little guilty too, but he's doing a great job covering it up with a big stupid smile on his face. He's steering the front of another tandem with Johnny Waterfall hanging off the back. They keep trying to do wheelies and are the frontrunners for Most Likely to Injure Themselves.

—

The town of Put-in-Bay is usually a pretty rowdy place—a place where men slowly transform into vented fishing shirts covered in vomit, women turn into broken pairs of flip-flops covered in Jose Cuervo, and everyone else finds a comfortable place to rest their head in between as some weird white dude with an unbuttoned Hawaiian shirt and a baby blue Cavs hat plays a remix of Bobby McFerrin's "Don't Worry Be Happy" on his CDJs.

But today's different. Because the ferries aren't really running, the town is quiet. I've never actually looked at the buildings on the island. Without the swarms of people and the noise, the strip is actually quite charming, and not very big at all. It feels something like New England. Not Maine, not Connecticut—maybe Rhode Island? A dusty Rhode Island. I don't know. I've never been to Rhode Island. It's probably nothing like that. It's really its own thing. It's Put-in-Bay, and it feels just like Put-in-Bay, and it's great. It doesn't need to be anything else. It doesn't need to be compared to New England. It's Ohio. This is what this part of Ohio looks like. And that's good.

The gang seems to be delighted by its charm. We're a gang of people riding bicycles through the street of a little lake town without a care in the world. Even Doobs seems to be letting his guard down, his pinstripe coat tails blowing in the breeze.

A Good Ol Fashioned Maritime

We get to the monument in almost no time at all—ten minutes, maybe. I think all of us anticipated the trip taking a little longer. If we really knew how close we were, I bet we'd have taken the long way around, but here we are, rolling up to the base of the monument, everyone, including Dave, collectively thinking, "What comes next?"

Honestly, I don't think any of us have a clue. And as concerning as that is, I think we're all at peace with it. We've gotten this far, after all.

Perry's Victory and International Peace Memorial is a big granite lighthouse-esque tower that stands over a grassy 25-acre park. It's 47ft taller than the Statue of Liberty and was constructed in honor of the people that fought in the Battle of Lake Erie during the War of 1812. I think there are actually some U.S. and British officers buried somewhere under the monument—which really seems to add to the disrespectful nature of us being here. But if you squint your eyes and pretend to think about it, is there a better way to honor the continued peace between the US, Canada, and Britain than to host a fake funeral for a living friend while listening to Rod Stewart? Sure, those Red Coats had a better Navy and yes, we were probably a little cocky in thinking we could just "liberate Canada" from Mother England, but that took balls, right? And it takes balls to throw a phony maritime funeral for a friend on federal property, right? This is a celebration of American balls.

As we dismount our steel steeds and lean them against the stone wall that surrounds the monument, I look to the Thompson twins, who "have it all worked out. Don't worry about it."

They both point towards a grassy knoll beyond the big stone monument. There, we see rows of folding chairs facing the water. Between them, a small podium and an arrangement of flowers.

"Jesus," Murphy says, still holding the giant framed photo of 'Fischer' under his arm. "The Thompson twins pulled it off." [37]

"*Damn straight!*" yells Travis from 40 yards away.

We look back at him, wondering how he could hear us from so far off. He waves.

As we walk through the muddy, snow-scattered grass towards the water, it begins to feel like a funeral processional again. But this time, we move in a bit of a mob rather than a line. The whole group, family included, begins to feel like a single unit rather than the pockets of people you find clustered at a funeral. We're all out of our element at this point, but there's a sense of camaraderie that comes with mutual improvisation.

Everyone seems to be going with the flow, the way you would at the funeral of a distant friend. Even the Thompsons, despite their heavy involvement with this portion of the festivities, seem to be playing it loose. I'm grateful for all their help in organizing the Put-in-Bay

---

[37] I don't know how he held onto this monstrosity while riding that bike. If there's a will there's a way.

portion of the day, but the fact that they seem to be as surprised as the rest of us is a bit concerning.

We settle into the folding chairs in an appropriate fashion: The family sits up front as the rest of us scatter about.

Tyler Thompson pulls out a little Bluetooth speaker and puts on the song, "Ooh La La" by the English rock group Faces. (It's a pretty charming song choice, really. Playful, nostalgic, heart-wrenching stuff.)

As I look around, everyone seems so at peace. Connie's had a big smile on her face since she got on that bicycle. I'm impressed with her willingness to go along with this stupid plan. I look around at the rest of the homies and I realize they're doing the same thing. I think we're all pretty impressed with ourselves—an emotion we're not really used to. It's a good feeling. All of us sitting there together feels more like a wedding. It feels celebratory. It feels like we *did* something. We got all the way here. We faked a death. We threw a wake. We (accidentally) threw a parade. We got on a ferry and now we're sitting by the water, pretty pleased with ourselves.

As we exchange polite smiles back and forth underneath the Rod Stewart's vocal fry, a light chatter and darkness sweeps the crew. My brain begins to hunt for a reason as to why the tone could be changing so abruptly. Then I realize that I'd completely forgotten about Dave—the reason we're trying to pull off this bullshit in the first place.

Bringing back the fact that all of this is aimed at Dave really dilutes the feeling of pride in doing something so extravagant. Just for a second, it felt like we were doing something cool for the sake of doing it. I imagine this is the feeling artists and musicians are chasing on a regular basis.

No one makes art or music *just* to spite people. Creating things out of spite is more of a modern right-wing political motivation. Nothing good comes from negative source material. Bringing someone else down doesn't raise you up, it leaves you in the same place.

As much fun as it is to plan an over-the-top comedy/revenge plot against a selfish dumbass like Dave, when that joyous camaraderie is replaced with the reality of negatively affecting another person, it sucks.

I notice that Dave isn't sitting with Kelsey. He's sitting a row in front of me, almost by himself, hunched over, tears in his eyes. On the other side of this block of cold, plastic folding chairs, Kelsey sits in front of me, next to Meghan.

The game of telephone sweeping the gang eventually gets to me. Johnny Waterfall leans into Ginger, who tells him something. Johnny mutters the word "Damn," then leans towards me. I lean in.

"Kelsey gave Dave the ring back," he says.

"What?" I ask, hoping I misunderstood.

"Yeah...pretty harsh."

I lean over to peak at Kelsey's hand, as she's sitting a row in front of me. Sure enough, no ring.

"Dammit," I say.

"Ooh La La" wraps up and the Thompson's funeral playlist goes into Prince's "Let's Go Crazy," the first track on the Purple Rain soundtrack. A jarring choice for a funeral, but very literal if you listen to the opening lyrics, I guess. I suppose it's appropriate enough for our current circumstances.

Then we hear what sounds like an ATV in need of an oil change. It's humming at a very loud and metallic frequency—a tone usually reserved for lawnmowers.

The small crowd turns to see Donnie's hearse slowly turning a corner of the park. The car seems to be smoking the way it was when we saw Dave and Donnie sitting in the gravel lot of the ice cream place.

As it approaches us, the smoke starts to get darker.

"Yeah, that's not great," says Josh-Josh.

The hearse continues up onto the grass, something it's definitely not supposed to do.

It continues to creep towards us and everyone seems to go on high alert, despite its slow pace. As it gets closer and closer, we stand and start to move away from it, folding up our chairs and taking them with us.

The hearse eventually stops about 25 yards past where we were originally sitting. Donnie opens the door and jumps out of the car, coughing as black smoke envelops the car.

"Ithinthersofiya!" he yells, coughing and running from the hearse.

"WHAT?!" shouts Dave.

"*Ithinthersa fiyaa*!" yells Donnie, coughing again.

"I think he's saying that there's a fire," ventures Meghan, as flames start to creep up the hood of the car.

Everyone turns to run, folding chairs in hand, as we finally realize what "taking it too far" looks like.

As the gang gets a good half of a football field away, Doobs and I turn to see Dave standing between us and the burning car.

"Dave," yells Doobs. "let's go!"

"I can't let Fish go out like this!" he yells back.

"Goddammit!" I say, looking at Doobs.

"Let's go, Dave! *The car's on fire!"* he yells.

Dave turns and looks back at the car, then back at us, then back at the car.

"This stupid motherfucker," says Doobs.

Dave takes off towards the flames, Doobs takes off after him, and I after Doobs. I've never seen Doobs run before. He's a pretty big guy, but as it turns out, he's fast as hell when he wants to be—either that, or he had some of that mother-lifting-a-car-off-of-her-child adrenaline going.

He catches up with Dave 20 yards from the car, picks his ass up, and turns around in one fell swoop, running with

Dave draped across his shoulders like you'd see in a war movie.

"*Go!*" Doobs screams at me. "*She's gonna blow!*"

Dave jumps off of Doobs's back and starts running from the flaming car on his own.

The hearse explodes into a black and orange gasoline fire, throwing Doobs and Dave to the ground, just like in the movies. I run and pull them both off the ground and we scurry away, hunched over, flames raging behind us.

We get back to the gang just as the Put-in-Bay fire department pulls up. The whole gang and some random onlookers are standing by the round stone bench that wraps around the base of the monument, watching the flames. The Fischers and my family stand there in awe of what just happened. Kelsey and Connie are crying and holding each other. The seersucker boys and Meghan are just standing there, heads cocked, mouths ajar, trying to comprehend the wildness. Murphy and Josh-Josh are standing side by side, arms crossed, each of them with one of their hands covering their mouth, laughing nervously. Donnie's sitting on the bench, smoking an old lady cigarette.

Kelsey runs up and hugs Dave.

"What the fuck is wrong with you?"

"I'm so sorry, babe. I'm sorry for *everything*," he says the way he's seen dialog like this play out in the movies.

He then turns to Doobs, while holding onto Kelsey.

“Doobs…you…you saved my life,” he says, again very cinematically.

“Fuck you, Dave,” says Doobs, still trying to catch his breath.

Then we hear another metallic, lawnmowery sound in the distance.

We turn to see, driving the long way around the flames and firetrucks, a weird little man with a stupid beard and a stupid hat riding a silver moped. I lower my head, laughing to myself, recognizing that timing is everything. There’s nothing like a poorly timed joke—especially one this extravagant.

The man pops his scooter up onto the sidewalk, similar to the way the hearse got up onto the grass (though thankfully less threatening).

He attempts to dramatically slide the scooter to a stop like a cool motorcycle guy, but he wobbles the steering and almost lays the bike down instead. He recovers, puts down the kickstand, turns off the scooter, and approaches us, the flames from the fire reflecting off of his stupid sunglasses.

“Hey, young man,” he says, approaching Dave. “I’m looking for the funeral of Arthur Fischer, the local man who died prematurely of natural causes.”

A collective groan rumbles through the small crowd as everyone is flabbergasted at the lack of tact on Fischer’s part.

"Hey, man. Yeah...this is it. Or, I guess, this *was* it," says Dave.

"How did you know him?" asks the man.

Another groan rumbles through the crowd, everyone shaking their heads as they realize that this grand finale is so, so stupid.

"Well...Fish was one of my nearest, dearest friends. He meant the world to me. Me and my beautiful bride-to-be were devastated to hear of his passing from natural causes," Dave says, gesturing to Kelsey. "So young. Such a loss."

People are becoming audibly upset at this point. If this were a Cleveland Browns game, people would be throwing things onto the field.

"Well, I'm sorry for your loss, my friend, but what if I told you that your tears of sadness would soon turn to tears of joy as I..." the man begins to remove his stupid disguise, "Arthur Fischer, am the man you see before you today!"

"Fish!" Dave says, hugging him casually. "I'm so happy to see you. Missed you, man!"

The crowd looks around. Everyone was expecting a much more chaotic and rage-filled response. They all look around, confused. There is silence.

Fischer breaks the pause.

"I said, it is I, Arthur Fischer, back from the grave. We've tricked you, Dave. This...this was a *prank*, and you have fallen for it. I understand if you are very upset with us because you were made a fool. But we have gotten you. Best prank ever, no doubt."

I pull Fischer to the side as people start to groan and mumble amongst themselves. "Are you completely sauced?" I ask him quietly.

"I got nervous," he says. "I've never revealed that I've faked my own death before. So yeah, I had like 6 beers at the bar while y'all were lollygagging with the damn bicycles."

"Why isn't he mad?" I ask. "I don't think he's even surprised."

"I know," he says. "I fully expected to get punched in the face."

Dave breaks our sidebar.

"Guys, I've got something to tell you."

We all stand and look nervously at each other.

"So...Kelsey and I aren't getting married."

I start to try to say something, but Kelsey stops me.

"And it's not what you think," she says.

"Yeah. Kelsey and I pretended to get engaged to mess with you guys," says Dave.

We pause and look at each other, again.

"We knew that if we got engaged, you guys would use it as an excuse to get the gang back together and pull off some elaborate shit just to mess with us," says Kelsey. "But you guys never planned anything. We were fake-engaged for almost 18 months and you guys didn't do shit."

"So, we came up with this bachelor party plan, hoping that would put you dummies to work. But once we heard about Fischer 'dying from natural causes,' we thought 'This must be it.' So…it was game on."

"So, you guys aren't engaged?" asks Ginger.

"Hell no!" says Kelsey. "You think I'd marry this idiot?"

"Easy," protests Dave. "You saw my performance with the 'she gave the ring back' thing."

"That was my fucking idea," Kelsey says.

"But I smoked it! I was crying and shit."

"I saw him," interjects Connie. "He was crying and everything."

"Mom!" says Fish.

"What? They did a great job! That was like real Broadway stuff. Your acting sucks, Arty. And you smell drunk."

"*Mom!*" repeats Fish. "Why you gotta be mean?"

"I'm just saying. I mean, I knew what was going on the whole time, but I really hoped your acting chops would be a little better. That big reveal was *really* bad."

"Dammit, Mom."

"Seriously though, dude. It was really bad," agrees Josh-Josh.

"Well sorry, I'm not some California actor type," says Fish.

"I'm just so glad you guys put forth the effort. I was really impressed," says Kelsey. "I mean…you guys got the Thompson twins involved! You got a parade going!"

"Yeah!" says Dave. "You got that weird dude with the exploding hearse. You got Doobs to *save* me!"

"That's right! That was the best part! Where is our hero?" Kelsey asks, looking around.

We all turn to look for Doobs.

"Oh fuck!" says Murphy. "Doobs! You all right?"

Doobs is sitting on the ground, holding his chest, his back leaning on the granite tower of Perry's International Victory and Peace Memorial.

"You all right, bud? You're going to get your suit all messed up."

Back on the Mainland

It's a chilly Friday afternoon in April, seven days after Fischer's funeral.

We've had pretty good weather this week, but it's snowing in April, again. I put Prince's "Sometimes It Snows in April" on the radio, but turn it off, as it feels too on the nose.

I pull into the parking lot of the weird old funeral home across from St. Pat's. I see Dave and Kelsey getting out of their car. They stand there in the cold and wait for me to catch up. They look good. It's kind of a shame that they're not really together. They look good together.

We walk across the street to the church and see the seersucker boys, in muted greys today, standing in the cold, talking and periodically blowing into their hands for warmth.

"Hey, guys," says Kelsey.

The guys respond with nods. We all awkwardly group hug and walk inside. We find some seats near the back of the church as we would on any other occasion where we'd enter a church.

Mrs. DuBois is standing in the front of the sanctuary, leaning on a pew and talking to some family members. (I assume they're family members. All of them look just alike.)

She catches our glances and waves for us to come closer to the front. We look at each other, reluctantly stand, and head up the aisle. Mrs. DuBois meets us halfway.

"I don't want you guys to feel awkward, but don't sit *all* the way in the back. You guys are family. Daniel loved you guys, and I know he's looking down and laughing at you having to deal with me telling you where to sit."

"Love you, Mrs. Doobs," says Pop.

"Yeah. Let us know if we can do anything," says Ginger.

She nods and smiles lovingly. She has no resentment for us at all—not visibly, at least.

I look around the church. I see Meghan and her mom wander in. I see my folks and parents of some other buddies. I see the Thompson twins and other randos from high school that I'd completely lost touch with. It's a funny bunch, but a loving one.

As I start to try and guess who's who and what relation they are to Doobs, I realize we're all a bunch of weirdos. There are people as disgusting as Meghan's Uncle Donnie. There are people as civil as Mrs. Doobs. On paper, there's no reason those two people should ever be in the same room, but here we are.

The funniest things in places like Northwest Ohio are the nuances. From an outsider's perspective, all these people may seem pretty mild, but after spending time with them, you realize that even the normiest of normies are beautifully strange and complex in their own ways.

There's space for those nuances in a place like this.

In coastal cultural Meccas, it's easy to find yourself in a scene of things. You adapt and shift with the times because something new crosses your path every single day. But because of that constant newness, you never have time to settle into a cozy space. You may become comfortable with that level of variety, and you have to keep hustling to pay that rent, but eventually, you have to carve out a space for peace amongst the chaos. If you can do that, the city can work for you.

But in Northwest Ohio, it's the inverse. In a space so quiet, so lost in its own sense of time, you have to build your own culture. You have to make your own variety. You have to discover your particular sense of self and build the things that you want to experience day-to-day. If you don't, then you'll get swept up in the path of least resistance—a passive-aggressive plague that dominates this part of the world. But if you can rise to the occasion, if you have a vision, if you have a way to combat the temptation of submitting to the mild norms of such a steady place, then the great Midwest can work for you.

As I sit here, I think, "Hey! Maybe that's me. Maybe *I* should move home."

I know these people. I like these people. They're funny and they never try to be. Every time I leave, my face hurts from laughing so much. Why wouldn't I move home?

I could open a business here. I could start a family here. I could bring something new to the table. There's space for something new here.

But new isn't always good. It's the old stuff that's good—especially back home.

Now, that's not to say that I don't enjoy the new brewery that pops up in the old body-shop or the little coffee shop they put inside that house on the corner, but when I go back home, I'd rather go to the old cinderblock ice cream shop. I'd rather go to the library. I'd rather go to Shoes.

Maybe that makes me an old man. I used to like new stuff. I used to keep up with new music and go to the new restaurants. Hell, I probably moved away because I was subconsciously looking for something new. Maybe that's the reason we all move away.

Now that I'm not looking for new things, I find myself looking for old things, things that feel like home. And if you're looking for things that feel like home, "back home" is a pretty good place to start.

As I start to weigh the pros and cons of something like a move back home, I realize that the most appealing quality of 'back home' is my personal memory of 'back home.' And memory's weird. Memory loves a good narrative. It loves a good story. And it's happy to overemphasize or redact all sorts of information—good or bad—whatever the story needs.

Most of my better memories involve the people sitting next to me in this church, and most of these people don't live here anymore either. So, while the concept of moving back home sounds appealing, I realize that my day-to-day wouldn't involve these weirdos any more than it does now.

And I think that's really what I'm chasing. I'm chasing the sense of camaraderie that I've felt over the past month, organizing a fake funeral. I'm chasing a sense of family-style friendship that only really exists in 90s sitcoms. I just happen to associate that time of life with Northwest Ohio.

I come to peace with this as my attention is brought back to the present. The double doors of the annex of the church open to reveal The DuBois Family, Fischer, and Murphy.

Everyone stands, and I'm overwhelmed with the weight of how strange life is. I'm devastated, but I'm also overwhelmed with a sense of family. What a bizarre group of people. What a beautiful mess. What a comically tragic circumstance.

But that's what life is. That's what home is. It's bizarre. It's beautiful. It's tragic. It's grey unless it's not. It's as wild and devastating as you want it to be.

It's a group of strangers singing in a bar. It's a parade for no reason. It's a van full of friends driving to the beach in the snow. It's a smoldering haunted house hearse overlooking Lake Erie.

Or sometimes, it's a lady playing an organ rendition of the Bonnie Tyler song, "Total Eclipse of the Heart" while your friends walk your other buddy's casket down the aisle. It's the occasional bursts of laughter coming from his family because irony's always funny.